For the Vegetarian in You

For the Vegetarian in You

Billy Ray Boyd

PRIMA PUBLISHING

This book is in no way intended to be medical advice for individual conditions. For that, you should consult a qualified healthcare practitioner of your choice—naturopath, homeopath, allopath, herbalist, acupuncturist, or holistic medical doctor—bearing in mind that even practitioners in the same discipline may disagree about the cause of particular symptoms and the recommended remedy, and that the choice of practitioners and therapies is yours. (See the DataBank at the end of this book for a list of national organizations of various therapeutic modalities.) Responsibility for any adverse effects resulting from the use of information in this book rests solely with the reader.

© 1996 by Billy Ray Boyd

PRIMA PUBLISHING and colophon are trademarks of Prima Communications, Inc.

Library of Congress Cataloging-in-Publication Data

Boyd, Billy Ray
 For the vegetarian in you / Billy Ray Boyd.
  p.   cm.
 Previously published: San Francisco, CA: Taterhill Press, 1987.
 Includes index.
 ISBN 0-7615-0123-1
  1. Vegetarianism.   I. Title.
RM236.B68 1995
613.2'62—dc20   95-31378
                                                                      CIP

95 96 97 98 99 AA 10 9 8 7 6 5 4 3 2 1
Printed in the United States of America

How to Order:
Single copies may be ordered from Prima Publishing, P.O. Box 1260BK, Rocklin, CA 95677; telephone (916) 632-4400. Quantity discounts are also available. On your letterhead, include information concerning the intended use of the books and the number of books you wish to purchase.

Contents

DataBank

The Vegan Vision

by Joanna Macy

I took a walk on the beach below the oil refineries on San Francisco Bay. Seagulls careened in the afternoon sun. A tanker hooked up a half-mile out on the jetty.

As I watched idly, a strange fantasy arose in my mind. It was a scenario of what would happen if Americans no longer found animal products attractive. Say they simply woke up one day and found meat and poultry and dairy products unappealing. Given U.S. eating habits, that speculation borders on the absurd, I know. But suppose some magical transformation took place that would diminish our attraction to animal-based foods, and at the same time increase our appetite and enjoyment for other foods which really nourish, and are far better for us.

What would happen? What would it mean for our lives and our world? Would that tanker, for example, still be making its deliveries of imported oil? Would those refineries stretch back for as many miles as they do now? Would there be as much DDT in the gulls overhead or in my own body? Would they and I be likely to live longer and healthier? From the evidence accrued in hundreds of recent medical, agricultural, economic and environmental studies, we can indeed estimate the results if Americans were to change their eating habits and kick the habit of over-consuming animal proteins and animal fats. I imagine then the scenario, as I walk along the water's edge.

The effects on our physical health are immediate. The incidence of cancer and heart attack, the nation's biggest killers, drops precipitously. So do many other diseases now demonstrably and causally linked to consumption of animal proteins and fats, such as osteoporosis, a major affliction among older women; my mother suffers from it; I fear it. The hormonal imbalances causing miscarriages and increasing aberrations of sexual development similarly drop away, as we cease ingesting with our meat, poultry and milk the drugs pumped into our livestock. So do the neurological disorders and birth defects due to pesticides and other chemicals, as we begin to eat lower on the food chain where these poisons are far less concentrated. Mother's milk, where they concentrate in greatest intensity, becomes safe again; we can nurse our babies without fear. Since these toxins attack the gene pool itself, causing irreversible damage, the change in diet improves the health of my children's children's children and generations to come.

The social, ecological and economic consequences, as we Americans turn away from animal food products, are equally remarkable. We find that the grain we previously fed to fatten livestock can now feed five times the U.S. population; so we have become able to alleviate malnutrition and hunger on a worldwide scale. We discover what it is like for us to sit down to eat without feeling guilt. Once relieved of it, we realize how great was that burden, that unspoken sense of being watched and judged by those who were hungry. We find ourselves also relieved of fear.

For on a semiconscious level we knew all along that the old disparities in consumption were turning our planet into a tinder box, breeding resentments and desperations that could only eventuate in war. We breathe easier, letting ourselves be emotionally in touch again with all our brothers and sisters.

The great forests of the world, that we had been decimating for grazing purposes (that was, we discover, the major cause of deforestation), begin to grow again. Oxygen-producing trees are no longer sacrificed for cholesterol-producing steaks.

The water crisis eases. As we stop raising and grinding up cattle for hamburgers, we discover that ranching and factory farms had been the major drain on our water resources. The amount now available for irrigation and hydroelectric power doubles. Meanwhile, the change in diet frees over 90 percent of the fossil fuel previously used to produce food. With this liberation of water energy and fossil fuel energy, our reliance on oil imports declines, as does the rationale for building nuclear power plants.

As expenditures for food and medical care drop, personal savings rise—and with them the supply of lendable funds. This lowers the interest rates, as does the drop in oil imports, which eases the pressure on the national debt.

A less obvious effect of our meat-free diet, but perhaps more telling on the deep psychological level, is the release that it brings from the burden of guilt of cruelty inflicted on other species. Only a few of us had been able to face directly the obscene conditions we inflicted on animals in our factory farms and modern slaughter houses; but most of us knew on some level that they entailed a suffering that was too much to "stomach."

We can appreciate now what it did to us to eat animals kept long in pain and terror. Because the mass methods employed to raise and kill animals for our tables were relatively new, we did not fully realize the deprivation and torture they entailed. Only a few of us guessed that the glandular responses of the cattle and pigs and chickens pumped adrenalin into their bodies and that we ate with their flesh the rage of the chickens, the terror of the pigs and cattle. It is good for our bodies, our relationships, and our politics to have stopped ingesting fear and anger. Acting now with more respect for other beings, we find we have more respect for ourselves.

As I picked my way over the shale and driftwood, I thought to myself, "This scenario is wildly, absurdly utopian. It is also clearly the way we are meant to live, built to live." There is a new way of living taking birth in our time. I encounter it everywhere I go in this land, in cities and small towns, in churches and schools, where folks are fed up with violence and disease and alienation, where they are creating new forms, new lifestyles, determined to live in ways that lend meaning and sanity to their lives. This new way takes seriously the values of individual dignity, freedom and justice that were heralded at the birth of our nation. It wants to share these values with all beings—knows it must share them in order to survive. It is fed up with consuming over half the world's resources; it is sick of being sick.

That is why, I suspect, the fantasy that occurred to me on the beach may not be so unrealistic.

Copyright ©1995, by Joanna Macy

Acknowledgments

I am indebted to friends, teachers, and allies too numerous to mention for their various gifts of advice, assistance, love, clarity, and encouragement. Among them are Clay Olson for his dedication in keeping this book alive and for being a friend when it wasn't easy, Sonika Tinker for primary education in emotional literacy, Regina Ryerson for taking time from her work and writing to give valuable insight and suggestions, the people with the Physicians Committee for Responsible Medicine who are transforming the way we perceive our dietary choices, and the millions of people who are living the vision now.

In apology to the trees cut down to make this book, and to the creatures who live among them, I can only say that every person who adopts a total vegetarian way of eating saves an acre of trees per year, allowing more trees and animals to live while themselves enjoying greater personal health and integrity.

Please let me know if this book affects your life. Write Billy Ray Boyd, P.O. Box 100-P, Santa Cruz, CA 95063-0100. Personal letters only, please—no bulk mailings.

For the Vegetarian in You

1

Introduction

G uns, hunting dogs primed for blood, the crisp air of autumn mornings, the camaraderie of my male companions, these constituted a rite of passage from boyhood into manhood in my native Ozark mountains. I loved the smell of the trees, the feel of the ridges and hollows. The excitement of the hunt—"buck fever"—was a welcome relief from a life lived within walls and towns.

Yet the actual killing disturbed me. The hardest part was finishing off a downed animal, bleeding from bullet wounds, exhausted from the chase, facing death. Try as I might, I could neither ignore nor forget the fearful look in those pleading eyes. In this way, I learned that every creature values her or his life just as much as I value mine. Although I continued to hunt for a time, I was already a dormant, would-be vegetarian. I lacked the nutritional information, emotional support, and moral courage to act on my most fundamental feelings and intuitions.

Then I went away to college. I stopped hunting, but continued to eat meat, as much out of habit as from the belief—held by everyone I knew—that meat was necessary for a long and healthy life. I didn't know that most "food" animals suffered much more than the free animals I'd hunted, and except for vague references to mysterious religious groups, I didn't even know *of* anyone who was vegetarian. I certainly had no idea that I might actually be healthier if I didn't eat meat.

My feeling of isolation began to dissipate when I read an interview with comedian and antiwar activist Dick Gregory. Asked why he wouldn't burn down a building or kill a soldier to try and stop the Vietnam war, he didn't quote Gandhi or Martin Luther King. Instead, he answered with a dietary analogy. "I'll tell you I think eating meat is wrong," he said, "but I won't knock a steak out of your hand."

I was astounded to discover that there was another real, live person out there who actually felt as I did about killing animals. The fact that I already respected this person for his antiracism humor and antiwar activism only increased the impact of my discovery. I went straight to the kitchen and tossed out my frozen hamburger patties. I believed then that my health would suffer as a result and, in fact, at first my new way of eating wasn't the healthiest in the world: I remember eating lots of white macaroni and cheese because it gave me the same "full" (heavy) feeling in my stomach that meat had. But as I learned how to prepare more nutritious and tasty vegetarian foods, my sense of well-being actually improved, to my happy surprise. That hamburger toss over thirty years ago was my first step into ethical and healthful eating, a step that, despite the occasional inconveniences, I have never regretted.

"A journey of ten thousand miles," the ancient saying goes, "begins with the first step." The step into vegetarianism is much easier to make now than it was just a few decades ago, thanks to more widespread nutritional knowledge and greater acceptance of individuality in diet. More and more vegetarian dishes are appearing on restaurant menus, vegetarian prepared foods dot supermarket shelves and frozen food sections, and vegan (total-vegetarian) meals are spreading rapidly to university campuses and dormitories. Even in my hunter-culture hometown of just over a thousand souls, I'm now able to put together a satisfying meal in the cafeteria on the town square.

Still, "going veggie" can be a major decision, and even a scary one. A lot of people would like to take the step, but some don't know exactly what vegetarianism is. It's easy to get confused by the health claims of various diets, and learning to prepare satisfying plant-based meals does take some time and effort. This book aims to help you make your first step—or your next one—in the exciting and rewarding journey into new realms of healthful, pleasurable eating and humane living.

One book can't say everything there is to be said about the subject. Rather, the purpose of this book is to give you lots of basic information and to whet your appetite to learn more. It covers the various reasons for a vegetarian diet[1]— from personal and planetary health to world hunger, animal rights, and how it affects your sexuality—and it addresses your legitimate health and social concerns about this way of eating. In the DataBase of appendices at the end, you'll find interesting and useful information, whether you're new to it all or a seasoned vegetarian.

2

Well-Defined

Being a vegetarian doesn't mean avoiding chemical additives in food, however wise and good that may be, nor is organically grown chicken a vegetarian food! It also doesn't necessarily mean being "New Age" or into yoga or having an Indian guru; you don't have to take on any belief system or lifestyle to be vegetarian. Quite simply, *vegetarianism* means living without eating fish, non-plant seafood, birds, or other animals. Someone once put it this way: "I don't eat anything that tries to get away!" (Even mussels and clams try to avoid pain and death.)

The basic, purest form of vegetarianism is *veganism*, which involves living solely from the plant world—fruits, vegetables, grains, beans, nuts, and seeds, and anything made from these basic foods—as well as avoiding the use of all animal (including bird and insect) products such as leather, wool, silk,or down, as much as possible. Someone who eats only plant foods but uses other animal products such as leather or down is a *total vegetarian* or *dietary vegan*. The correct pronunciation of vegan is "VEE-gn," but so many people are going vegan without ever hearing the word that two new variations have sprung up: "VE-jn" (rhymes with "hedgin'") and "VAY-gn" (rhymes with "pagan"). This latter pronunciation can also refer to someone from Las Vegas, while the former sounds like "veggin'" as in "vegging out," with couch potato connotations. This might be used to support using the official (original) pronunciation "VEE-gn," which seems to sound sharp and harsh to American ears; I know it did to me when I first started using it, but now it seems normal.

If you modify a plant-based diet by including milk (lacto-) or eggs (ovo-) or both, then you are a *lacto-* or *ovovegetarian*. Most vegetarians in the United States are lacto- or lacto–ovovegetarians, though veganism is rapidly on the rise, especially among animal rights activists, teens, and college students. About twelve million people in the U.S. consider themselves vegetarians, up from seven million just eight years ago.

veg • e • tar • i • an \ ˌve-jə-'ter-ē-ən \ *n*
*(veget*able + *-arian)* **1:** one who lives solely on vegetables, fruits, grains, legumes, nuts, and seeds, with or without eggs or milk products. **2:** HERBIVORE

A *total* vegetarian is someone who eats no animal products at all (i.e., someone who is a dietary vegan), while the term *strict* refers simply to the consistency with which you follow whatever dietary path you choose to follow (vegan, lacto-vegetarian, or whatever). For example, a strict vegetarian never eats fish or fowl, but is not necessarily vegan, whereas a strict vegan is one who sticks strictly to veganism. Those of us who have bad associations with the word "strict" (perhaps because of having had an overly strict disciplinarian for a parent or teacher) can substitute the word *consistent*, describing ourselves as consistent vegetarians or vegans.

With the increasing acceptance of nonstandard eating patterns in the U.S. over the last few decades, the meaning of the word vegetarian has become fuzzy. Some people mistakenly believe that eating limited quantities of chicken or fish or abstaining from red meat makes them vegetarian. It doesn't. For lack of a better term, they're called *semi-* (or part-time) *vegetarians*. They differ from the general population by limiting the types or quantity of flesh foods they eat and the frequency with which they eat them. Semi-vegetarians have increased in numbers even more rapidly than vegetarians. They may be wishful thinkers, backsliders from more idealistic days, or in transition to a more healthy, ecological, and humane way of eating; or they may feel they've struck a workable compromise between ideals, habit, and social custom, a compromise that may or may not shift at a later time. A portion of the twelve million people in the U.S. who say they are vegetarian are undoubtedly semi-vegetarians. The positive image of vegetarianism is leading more and more people to jump on the bandwagon, and an increasing number of those who still eat meat want to be *seen* as vegetarian, or at least vegetarian-*ish*. There are even cookbooks on the market for people who are *almost, sort of, sometimes,* or *mostly* vegetarian.

An enticing array of food philosophies beckons to the new vegetarian. To name just a few, *raw food* folks consider uncooked foods to be most compatible with our bodies and the most ecological and fuel efficient (no energy used in cooking or processing). *Living foods* advocates not only eat it raw, they eat it live: foods like sprouts and living-culture fermented drinks. *Macrobiotics*, which promotes a grain-based, mostly cooked diet (not necessarily vegetarian, but it's often vegan), claims that human cultural evolution began with the discovery of fire and the cooking of food, as evidenced by the grain-based diets of all cultures throughout history. Many vegetarians, however, simply follow their *standard cultural fare* and "vege-tarianize" whatever they're already used to, substituting veggie burgers for hamburgers, roasting wheat gluten instead of pork chops, ordering pepperoniless pizzas, and scarfing down soy hot dogs.

There are endless variations on these basic themes. As a new vegetarian, you would be well advised to enter this confusing but exciting world with a spirit of both adventure and skepticism. Instead of casting yourself down at the feet of some dietary guru or swallowing whole the first food philosophy that comes your way, listen to various ideas and viewpoints, try an assortment of foods prepared in a variety of ways, and listen to what your body, your mind, and your heart are telling you. In other words, honor your history and respect your own physical and mental ecology.

Granted, listening to your body's wisdom isn't always as easy as it sounds. We're so conditioned to unhealthy things that what *seems* to be a real physical need is often a habit or addiction in disguise. Learning to tell the difference between natural, health-promoting desire on the one hand (carrot juice after a workout) versus unhealthful conditioning on the other (those sugar and fat cravings) may be a lifelong task. There's no better time to begin than now.

3

Vege-Vitality

*One farmer says to me, "You cannot live on veg-
etable food solely, for it furnishes nothing to make
bones with," and so he religiously devotes a part of
his day to supplying his system with the raw material of bones; walking all the while he talks behind
his oxen, which, with vegetable-made bones, jerk
him and his lumbering plow along in spite of every
obstacle.*

HENRY DAVID THOREAU

It wasn't very long ago at all that vegetarians had to argue
with concerned friends and family that vegetarian foods
were nutritionally adequate. Medical and dietary publications issued dire warnings about the dangers of vegetarian
diets, or at best fretted about how important "careful planning" was in order to avoid nutritional deficiencies for
adults; raising children vegetarian was considered a degree of irresponsibility bordering on child neglect.

This has changed dramatically in the last few decades, as numerous medical studies have shown plant-based foods to be not only adequate but nutritionally superior. Studies of Seventh Day Adventists (a vegetarian Christian sect) and others conducted over a number of years provide clear evidence of the health benefits of vegetarian—especially vegan—diets.

John McDougall, M.D., took the work of Nathan Pritikin, M.D., eliminated the animal products from the lowfat Pritikin diet, and showed impressive results; I first heard of him back in the 70s when I was living in Hawaii and several people I knew swore that they or their family members where "alive and healthy today because of Dr. McDougall," after having been given up as hopeless by other doctors.

More recently, work done by Dean Ornish, M.D., at the University of California, San Francisco Medical Center shook the medical community by showing that a vegan diet, along with exercise, relaxation techniques, and involvement of patients' companions could not only stop but actually reverse coronary heart disease, giving new meaning to the words of the Madonna song. "Open your heart."

Michael Klaper, M.D., has become "the vegans' doctor," in person and through his books on such subjects as vegan nutrition and child rearing. Suzanne Havala, a registered dietitian and a member of the American Dietetic Association, and others within the ADA organized to overcome the cautionary tone of the organization's attitude toward plant-based diets. And the massive China Diet and Health Study, conducted by prestigious American and Chinese universities, has examined the eating patterns and health of tens of thousands of rural Chinese people, most of whom by American standards have very few animal products in their diet; they eat a lot less protein in general, a lot less fat, and a lot more starch, and their health is a lot better than ours—except in regions where people eat more fats and animal products.

These results are driving the fatal spike into the heart of the meat-is-health Dracula, showing clearly the health benefits of a plant-based diet. People in positions of high nutritional authority now laud the virtues of a lowfat, plant-based diet, in stark contrast to what their predecessors were saying just two or three decades ago.

Even the National Live Stock and Meat Board, an industry propaganda group, admits the nutritional adequacy of a vegetarian diet. In their brochure "Meat and the Vegetarian Concept," they largely ignore the moral basis of vegetarianism and defend meat as a "more convenient" source of protein. But with meat proving to be a major contributor to the big killer diseases of our time, and considering it's actually harder to get a balanced diet *with* meat than *without* it, it's hardly a "convenient" source of anything except pain and suffering.

The health benefits of vegetarianism come in even greater abundance if you go vegan. The average meat-eating man in the United States has a 50 percent chance of having a heart attack, the most common cause of death in this country. A vegan man's chance of a heart attack is a mere 4 percent. A meat-eating woman is five times as likely to develop breast cancer as a vegan woman. Colon cancer is ten times higher in men and women who eat meat and dairy products than it is among vegans. Men's sperm count is down 30 percent from just a few decades ago, the most likely culprit being pesticide residues, which are much more highly concentrated in meat, eggs, and milk (including milk products like cheese) than in plant foods. And the babies—future adults—benefit, too, from our switch to a healthier diet. Ninety-nine percent of mothers' milk in the U.S. contains dangerous levels of DDT, but among vegan women, only 8 percent have dangerous levels. Again, this is because of the much higher concentrations of pesticides in animal products.

The sources of pesticides in our diet are[1]:

Meat (including fish and poultry)	51.9%
Dairy Products	20.7%
Oils and Fats	7.6%
Vegetables	8.5%
Fruits	5.0%
Legumes	4.8%
Grains	1.5%

Animal products formerly contained about 95% of the DDT in the diet (back when that agricultural poison was still legally used) and are the source of 90% of our dietary dioxin. So a vegan, even if eating chemically grown supermarket foods, takes in far less agricultural poison than someone who eats the Standard American Diet (SAD). That translates into less disease and better health.

But it's not only pesticides that make meat a killer. In Britain, a relatively new and deadly neurological disease, popularly called "Mad Cow Disease," has been killing thousands of cattle each year by eating up their brains. It's not pretty to watch the progress of the disease, as cows become disoriented and lose physical coordination, including the ability to stand up. No one knows for sure whether Mad Cow Disease is contagious to humans who eat the meat. Some companion animals ("pets") have reportedly contracted the disease from eating pet food made from infected cattle. Despite the British beef industry's assertions that its products are safe, beef consumption in the traditionally beef-eating United Kingdom dropped dramatically, and over 2,000 schools in that island nation no longer serve beef in school lunches; *all* schools there offer a vegetarian alternative lunch.

Mad Cow Disease was apparently spread by the practice—widespread in modern animal agriculture—of feeding ground-up dead animals to live ones, mixed in with their feed, which may also contain shredded newspaper, cement dust, feathers, sawdust, and processed sewage. With the uproar over Mad Cow Disease and with demand for beef plummeting, that practice was stopped in 1989 for British cattle. *If* Mad Cow Disease affects people, it will take an estimated twenty years—longer than the latency period for AIDS—for infected humans to begin to show symptoms, and there's no way to test for infection. As one BBC radio broadcast put it, "A whole generation of Britons [except, of course, vegetarians] may have been given a death sentence by eating beef infected with Mad Cow Disease." Several hundred live cattle were exported to the United States before the 1989 ban on feeding dead animals to live cattle, and a variant of the disease may already exist here.

But that may not be the end of the problem. Whether or not vegetarians will be the only survivors of a greatly depopulated Britain twenty or twenty-five years from now, the fear about this disease illustrates an important fact: Animal diseases are far more likely to be contagious to humans than are plant diseases. We may have variants of Mad Cow Disease over the coming decades, but no one's worrying about contracting "Mad Soybean Disease." And when the American Cancer Society, hardly a bastion of vegetarianism or animal rights (they fund painful experiments on animals), produced its poster of cancer-fighting foods, they included apple, artichoke, onion, banana, strawberry, collard greens, papaya, iceberg lettuce, tomato, broccoli, cantaloupe, kale, kiwifruit, kohlrabi, grapefruit, brussels sprout, orange, potato, bell pepper, prune, carrot, Swiss chard, spinach, apricot, avocado, acorn squash, savoy cabbage, celery, cauliflower, and sweet potato. Not one of the thirty beautiful, full-color pictures is of a steak, egg, glass of milk, or other animal product—they're all fruits and vegetables. (For a free copy, large or small size, contact your local branch of the American Cancer Society or call 800-422-6237 or 800-227-2345.)

Upton Sinclair's book *The Jungle*, published back in 1906, exposed the cruelty of the slaughterhouses and meat-packing plants for both animals and workers, and the unhygienic conditions under which the meat was processed. Sinclair himself was a vegetarian. Public pressure about the lack of good hygiene grew, but most people were concerned not so much about what happened to the animals as about what went into their own stomachs. In response, the government set up Department of Agriculture meat inspections, which we still have. Often, a lone inspector is assigned to guarantee the absence of disease in a constant and rapid stream of animal corpses on the disassembly lines of modern mechanized slaughterhouses. It's physically impossible to thoroughly inspect each carcass under such conditions, and for meat that's not sent across state borders, there's not even USDA inspection. So it's not surprising that about a third of all supermarket chicken meat is infected with salmonella, invisible to the eye.

Human beings are obviously "omnivore capable"; we can eat a wide variety of plant and animal foods. This flexibility has been of great help to our species in surviving the various historical epochs and often hostile environments—for example, the ice age, drought, and famine—and is something to be grateful for.

Nonetheless, our bodies much more closely resemble the herbivorous (plant eating) animals than the carnivorous (flesh eating) ones. Our intestines are twelve times our body length, while carnivores' are only three times theirs, allowing the rapidly decaying meat to leave their bodies quickly. We have blunt, not pointed, molar teeth and a jaw that can rotate for thorough chewing of grains and vegetables, rather than fangs for ripping and tearing of live or freshly killed raw flesh. We have flat nails and millions of pores in our skin, characteristics typical of herbivores; carnivores have claws, not nails, and no skin pores. In a pinch, we can eat other animals, but it's not what we were designed for. When our ancestors couldn't get enough to eat by just gathering food, they became hunter-gatherers. With our plentiful supply of food now, we can go back to the plant-based diet we're best suited for—and in the process (as we'll see later) help those who don't have enough to have more.

Youth is wonderful, fitness is healthy, and weighing more than we need to can keep us from functioning at our best. But our culture seems to make an unhealthy obsession out of these qualities. This can be oppressive both to those who don't fit the stereotypes (generating negative self-images) and to those who do (creating anxiety that they may lose their tenuous hold on being okay); in fact, some studies have indicated that "beautiful people" and especially those in the running may be less happy than those who have no chance of making the grade and are therefore more relaxed about it all. Even well-meaning health advice from vegetarians sometimes plays into this oppressive "looks-ism." Which is too bad, because there are plenty of benefits to being relatively trim to motivate us to take care of ourselves, without making ourselves or others feel bad for not fitting some health or beauty "authority's" ideal. Exercise and a healthy, lowfat, plant-based diet can help each of us gravitate naturally toward whatever weight is best for us.

4

Protein Pressure

It used to be that the most common question a new vegetarian was likely to get from friends or family was, "But what about protein?" Though the general pubic is better educated about protein these days, the question still gets asked, though less often now. In our society, there's a lot of pressure to "get enough protein."

Sufficient protein is essential for human life. It is not an energy food, as many people mistakenly believe. Energy is provided primarily by carbohydrates like grains, starchy foods, and fruits. (The body does convert protein into energy in nutritional emergencies, i.e., when there is insufficient carbohydrate or fat, or an excess of protein.)

Protein is essential for physical growth in children, and is the stuff used to rebuild blood cells and replace enzymes. It regulates the body's balance and distribution of fluids, helps maintain chemical neutrality, and is necessary in combating infection and disease. But our protein needs increase only a little, if at all, when we exercise or do hard physical work. According to the National Academy of

Sciences, "There is little evidence that muscular activity increases the need for protein." It is *carbohydrate* intake that must increase with physical exertion.

Proteins are composed of amino acids. Of the large total number of amino acids, there are eight that the body cannot manufacture on its own. These are called the *essential* amino acids, meaning we must get them in our food. The official human protein "requirement" was originally (and erroneously) determined by feeding rats varying amounts and combinations of amino acids to find out how much of which kinds kept them healthy. This seemed to many at the time to be good science, but there was a problem that comes up whenever animals are experimented on to try to learn about human physiology: There are major biological differences between species. For example, relative to body weight, baby rats require *ten times* as much protein as baby humans.

Over the last few decades, as we've learned more about human nutrition, the official scientific protein "requirement" has been repeatedly revised downward from the rat standard. The daily adult male allowance can be met with 3 ounces of peanuts, a bowl of split pea soup, two slices of whole grain toast, and a 10-ounce glass of soy milk—over the course of the whole day. The U.S. Recommended Daily Allowance (RDA) allows for a great deal of individual physiological variation. It is considerably above the actual requirements of most people, and the rat standard may well be further revised downward in the future. At any rate, a person eating the Standard American Diet gets about twice as much protein as she or he needs, even by conservative government standards. We Americans tend to think that if something's good, more is better, but excess protein can actually hurt us, for example by depleting our bones of calcium (more about that later).

Many plant foods are rich in protein. For example, chicken has no more protein than almonds (18.6%), and less than sunflower seeds (24.0%). Both garbanzo beans (chickpeas) (20.5%) and lentils (24.7%) exceed beef (20.2%). Soybeans (34.1%) outrank both beef and Swiss cheese (27.5%), with more than double the protein of lamb (16.8%).

Only part of this high protein rating for plant foods is accounted for by the high water content in meats compared with the dry weights given above for beans, seeds, and nuts. Powdered cow's milk, for example, is 26.4 percent protein, compared with powdered soybean milk at 41.8 percent, while the fat content in soy milk is considerably lower than in cow's milk.

Beans in general are very concentrated protein sources, and low in fat, while nuts and seeds are high in both protein and fat. High-protein *tofu*—pressed soybean curd, which takes on the flavors of foods it is cooked with—has immigrated from China and Japan, enriching vegetarian cuisine in the U.S. Although it has only recently gained widespread popularity here, it's been with us for a long time: it's a little-known fact that Benjamin Franklin made and ate tofu. This remarkably versatile food is now widely available in natural food stores and many super-markets, while *tempeh*, a cultured soy food originating in Indonesia, is still generally available only in natural food stores. Beans, seeds, and nuts can be made into delicious loaves, burgers, etc. All plant foods—unlike meat, milk, and eggs—are cholesterol free.

In our protein-obsessed society, vegetarians and meat eaters alike are encouraged to "play it safe," to eat protein far beyond their needs rather than take a chance on falling even slightly short of the official requirement. But when our bodies process excess protein into fuel (energy), diuretic nitrogen wastes are produced, resulting in leaching of calcium

and other minerals from the body. This contributes to osteoporosis, or weakening of the bones, especially common in
older women in high-protein societies like ours. What's
more, the leached calcium can form painful kidney stones.

High-protein diets also cause destruction of kidneys
and deterioration of kidney function. The concentrated
purines in high-protein foods break down into uric acid,
which collects in the joints causing gout, a severe type of
arthritis. As with many good things, more is not
necessarily better. So be kind to your kidneys, let your liver
live, and have joyous joints—go easy on *all* protein. Get
enough, but not too much.

While gluttony by any other name is still gluttony,
overeating plant protein is not as bad as overeating animal protein. Heart attacks, strokes, and sexual problems
are associated with meat eating, while biological concentrations of insecticides, industrial pollutants, and toxic
wastes are greater in animal products of all kinds
because animals are higher on the "bioconcentration"
food chain than are plants. As if that weren't bad enough,
animals grown in intensive-confinement "factory farms,"
as most are these days, have to be given increasingly
large doses of antibiotics and other drugs to prevent the
outbreak and rapid spread of epidemic diseases in their
overcrowded conditions. Considerable residues of these
dangerous drugs wind up in the meat, eggs, and milk in
your grocery store.

We'll talk more about protein later in this book, but for
now a closing note: You may read about "combining"
foods to maximize protein, and there are other people who
talk about "food combining" to maximize digestibility.
These are two entirely different things, and the use of the
term "combining" for both causes some confusion. For followers of Natural Hygiene, keys to health include sun-
shine, exercise, and proper diet. The ideal is uncooked
food eaten one type of food at a meal to maximize diges-

tion and nutrition, but if one combines various foods in a meal, then some combinations are better than others. This is combining foods for best digestion, and is different from combining foods to maximize protein utilization. So when you hear or read about food "combining," make sure it's clear which sort of combining is being talked about.

5

Gimme Four

The four basic food groups that most of us were raised with were the result of intensive lobbying by the meat and dairy industries. Many of us grew up viewing these food groups—meat, milk, starches, and (lumped together) fruits and vegetables—as a scientific (if not divine) scheme for classifying foods. But a glance at the history of food groupings reveals a different picture.

Until early in this century, there were *no* food groups. People ate what they had traditionally eaten, influenced much less than today by advertising. But with the increase in affluence, they ate more of the foods that traditionally they had eaten much smaller amounts of, namely animal foods and sweets. Then the government shifted its position and set forth *five* food groups: animal products (meat, milk, eggs, fish, etc.) and "meat substitutes" (i.e., vegetable protein sources), bread and grains, butter and healthy fats, vegetables and fruits, and sweets. During World War II, Americans were initially told to eat from *ten* food groups, and then a "Basic Seven" was declared, with one of the basic groups being fortified margarine and butter.

In 1954 we got the now-old Four Food Groups that most of us grew up with. Thanks to the influence of the meat and dairy industry, two of the four groupings were for animal products—the meat and milk groups—setting the stage for a major increase in meat and milk consumption, and therefore in diet-related diseases. Industry groups like the Dairy Council and the Egg Board came to be major suppliers of "educational" literature for public and private schools. They give their materials free to school districts that are often financially strapped. I've seen commercial intrusion into the classroom where I teach English to immigrants, with a company offering teaching materials featuring their products, language-development exercises in how to prepare their products, and samples to be given to the students, all "completely without charge;" in 1995 *Consumer Reports* ran an investigative article titled "Selling to School Kids."

They get 'em young, too. McDonalds advertises in *American Teacher*, the official publication of the American Federation of Teachers. One full-color, full-back-cover ad offers "nutritional information" in the form of "teaching aids" for kindergarten through third grade teachers, "to help guide your class to a healthier, more active lifestyle in a fun and interesting way." The message is clear: McDonalds stands for health and fun, and you read about it in the teachers' union magazine, so it must be okay.

Meanwhile, the Physicians Committee for Responsible Medicine (PCRM, see Appendix C: Organizations) came up with their own New Four Food Groups, based on studies in human nutrition that were pointing more and more strongly to the health hazards of animal products. They also provide menu-planning programs for large institutions and a range of educational materials, including "The

Right Bite" for classroom teachers, complete with masters for photocopying, giving teachers an alternative to the free "educational" materials offered by the likes of McDonalds and the Dairy Council.

In 1990, the government, bowing a little to the over-whelming scientific evidence against a meat-based diet, declared the old Four Food Groups obsolete and gave us its replacement—the Food Pyramid. Many people were perplexed: A cornerstone in our understanding of food and nutrition had suddenly been dislodged from our belief system.

While it's a somewhat positive reform from the old Four Food Groups, shifting emphasis *toward* grains, legumes, vegetables, and fruits, it stops far short of what would be a truly healthy dietary scheme. It can also be misleading. It places the *least* healthy foods at the *top* of the pyramid, which is narrower, meaning we should eat less of them. But this can give the impression that they're "tops," the best. Given the high level of functional illiteracy in the U.S. (a factor apparently not taken into account by the pyramid's designers), some people will probably get that impression. An inverted pyramid would have been more visually and psychologically accurate. Politically savvy observers suspected that the introduction of the Food Pyramid was a direct attempt by the government, under the influence of the animal products industry, to deflect growing public attention away from PCRM's dietary recommendations by putting forth this watered-down compromise.

If we look at what nutritional science is telling us, ignoring for a moment our cultural habits and the vested interests of the animal products industry, the PCRM's New Four Food Groups are not only healthier, but also a lot simpler:

This chart, the following explanation, and sample daily dietary guidelines are reprinted with the permission of the Physicians Committee for Responsible Medicine.

THE NEW FOUR
FOOD GROUPS

FOR OPTIMAL NUTRITION

Daily Servings

GRAINS
5 or more servings (1 serving—
1/2 cup hot cereal, 1 oz. dry cereal, 1
slice of bread, 1/2 cup cooked rice)

VEGETABLES
3 or more servings (1 serving—1 cup
raw or 1/2 cup cooked vegetables)

FRUITS
3 or more servings (1 serving—
1 medium piece of fruit, 1/2 cup fruit
juice)

LEGUMES
2–3 servings (1 serving—1/2 cup
cooked beans, 8 oz. soy milk)

Grains include bread, rice, pasta, hot or cold cereal, tortillas, corn, millet, barley, bulgur, and buckwheat groats. Build each of your meals around a hearty grain dish; grains are high in fiber and other complex carbohydrates, as well as protein, B vitamins, and zinc.

Vegetables are packed with nutrients; they provide vitamin C, beta-carotene, riboflavin, and other vitamins, iron, calcium, and fiber. Dark green, leafy vegetables such as broccoli, collards, kale, mustard and turnip greens, chicory or bok choy are especially good sources of these important nutrients. Dark yellow and orange vegetables such as carrots, winter squash, sweet potatoes, and pumpkin provide extra beta-carotene. Include generous portions of a variety of vegetables in your diet.

Fruits are rich in fiber, vitamin C, and beta-carotene. Be sure to include at least one serving each day of fruits that are high in vitamin C: citrus fruits, melons, and strawberries are all good choices. Choose whole fruit over fruit juices, which don't contain as much healthy fiber.

Legumes, which is another name for beans, peas, and lentils, are all good sources of fiber, protein, iron, calcium, zinc, and B vitamins. This group also includes chickpeas, baked and refried beans, soy milk, tofu, tempeh, and texturized vegetable protein.

Be sure to include a good source of vitamin B-12. If you're vegan, good sources are fortified whole grain cereals and vitamin supplements.

Daily Dietary Sample Guidelines

Food Group	Number of Daily Servings	Serving Size
Grains	5 or more	$1/2$ cup hot cereal 1 oz. dry cereal 1 slice of bread
Vegetables	3 or more	1 cup raw $1/2$ cup cooked
Fruits	3 or more	1 medium piece of fruit $1/2$ cup cooked fruit $1/2$ cup fruit juice
Legumes	2 to 3	$1/2$ cup cooked beans 4 oz. tofu or tempeh 8 oz. soy milk

6

Total Health

We are complex beings who do not live by food alone. For true health and happiness we need lots of things besides good food, like fresh air, exercise, love, physical touch, respect, challenge and cooperation, privacy and social connectedness, physical and psychological safety, stress release, meaningful work, a positive self-image, a sense of social and political relevance ("empowerment"), sexual expression, a degree of "emotional literacy"—knowing how to accept, express, and deal constructively with our feelings—and a need for some sort of inner development, discovery, or unfolding often described as "spiritual."

All these things influence each other. For example, exercise helps in the assimilation of food, while stress and unresolved emotional problems inhibit digestion, and social isolation can cause either overeating or loss of interest in food. If we don't get enough touch and love in our lives, we're likely to try to satisfy all our needs for them through sex, placing too many demands on it and thereby undermining sexual relationships. Knowing that our diet is non-violent improves our self-image, which in turn affects what we do in all areas.

Politics, including decisions made in centers of government, has a major impact on the quality of our air, water, and food, not to mention the chances for war and all the suffering and devastation that it brings. The very existence of nuclear, chemical, biological, and "conventional" weapons adds to the psychological toll taken by our daily diet of media violence—and, for many, real-life violence. While the end of the cold war has removed the immediate danger of massive nuclear war, our lives are being made *less* secure by the development of "leaner and meaner" nuclear first-strike systems, the unwillingness of the nuclear powers to disarm in exchange for the non-nuclear countries staying non-nuclear, the mushrooming black market in nuclear bomb materials from the stockpiles of the former Soviet Union, and the increasing possibility of "suitcase nukes" being used by terrorists.

Spending on preparations for war takes valuable resources from environmental, health, educational, and social programs. Regressive taxes (which hit low-income people proportionally harder than those in the upper incomes) and more government benefits to the rich than to the poor are making us into an increasingly economically undemocratic country, undermining our pride in the many positive aspects of our culture, as we vie for the dubious honor of incarcerating a greater proportion of our citizens than any country on earth. This all affects our mental health, how we feel about ourselves. In early 1995, it became official: in terms of the gap between rich and poor, the United States is the worst among all industrialized nations. A progressive breakdown of community, our infatuation with guns, an official economy based on violence (worldwide, the U.S. is responsible for 70 percent of all arms sales), and an emphasis on isolated "families" not rooted in healthy community does not make good soil in which healthy human beings can grow.

Gandhi was supposedly once asked by a reporter, "Sir, what do you think of Western civilization?" To which his reply was: "I think it would be a good idea."

Just as the gap between rich and poor is widening and the middle class is shrinking, we also seem to be experiencing a polarization along dietary lines. Although we're shifting in a vegetarian direction, the bottom isn't dropping out of the meat market; there are shifts from one kind of meat to another (beef to chicken and back again), but no precipitous decline overall. Apparently, as more and more people are eating less and less meat, others are eating more, clinging to the fading old-order image of meat and animal products generally as part of the "good life." This sort of increasing polarization often precedes a major cultural or political shift, as the issues are defined with increasing clarity.

The ecological teaching of our age, understood by many of the native peoples of the continent long ago, is that, in the words of Chief Seattle, leader of the Suquamish tribe, "everything is connected." The world is a complex place and we are affected by many things. It would be a mistake to think that good food alone will make us healthy and vibrant. Still, food, and the way we obtain it, is extremely important for our physical and mental well-being. While we may be more than what we eat, our personal and collective dietary choices do affect our thoughts, our behavior, and our self-esteem, as well as the world outside ourselves.

> *The white man must treat the beasts of this land as his brothers.*
>
> *I am a savage and do not understand any other way. I have seen a thousand rotting buffaloes on the prairie, left by the white man who shot them from a*

passing train. I am a savage and I do not understand how the smoking iron horse can be more important than the buffalo that we kill only to stay alive.

What is man without the beasts? If all the beasts were gone, men would die from a great loneliness of spirit. For whatever happens to the beasts, soon happens to man. All things are connected.

You must teach your children that the ground beneath their feet is the ashes of our grandfathers. So that they will respect the land, tell your children that the earth is rich with the lives of our kin. Teach your children what we have taught our children, that the earth is our mother. Whatever befalls the earth, befalls the sons of the earth. If men spit upon the ground they spit upon themselves.

This we know. The earth does not belong to man; man belongs to the earth. This we know. All things are connected like the blood which unites one family. All things are connected.

Whatever befalls the earth befalls the sons of the earth. Man did not weave the web of life; he is merely a strand in it. Whatever he does to the web, he does to himself.[1]

7

Vital Juices:
Vegetarianism and Sexuality

Sweeter kisses are [now] a reality . . .

A READER OF THIS BOOK

Meat often has a positive connotation in our culture. If something is "meaty," it's rich and substantive, while "vegging out" is to sit around passively, low in energy, like a couch potato. Getting to the "meat of the matter" means getting to the essential core. (A nice exception to this rule is the expression "meathead," referring to someone who is dull or stupid.)

Americans in general tend to feel that sex, especially *male* sexuality, is enhanced by eating meat. An article in *Playboy* magazine; "Men and Their Meat," presented this view blatantly, with a photo of a steak being cooked by a handheld blowtorch; favorite meat dishes and recipes of well-known men were described. A plant-based diet may be healthy, but if it's going to make us into sexless wimps, few people are going to be interested.

This association is not limited to Americans. Once, a number of years ago, as I was walking through a street market in Taiwan with a nonvegetarian Chinese friend, the conversation turned mildly ribald. After a few minutes of this banter, she stopped, turned and looked at me, and said: "You know, Billy, you're strange—you're vegetarian, but you think and talk about sex." In her mind, vegetarianism was associated with Buddhism, which in turn was associated not only with vegetarianism but with abstinence from all objects of lust and pleasures of the flesh.

The Chinese cultural belief that animal products vitalize vital energy sidetracks many a would-be vegetarian when an acupuncturist or Chinese herbalist prescribes small amounts of meat or other animal products. This is not surprising, since Chinese society shares with ours an obsession with animal products, though not in the same quantities. Where there is an addiction or a cultural habit, there are rationalizations to support it. (Vegetarian-friendly practitioners of Chinese medicine can, however, be found; when looking for one, ask in advance what their attitude is toward animal products in the diet.)

But back to our question: Does meat eating improve your sex life? The answer is: No, it undermines it, both indirectly and directly. First, the indirect effects.

In general, the worse your health—the more aches and pains you have and the lower your energy level—the less you're going to be interested in sex, and the less endurance you're going to have. You may find your passionate grappling inhibited by creaky joints gone arthritic because of the arachidonic acid in animal foods, and any number of other conditions might distract you from amorous pursuits, such as cancer of the colon and rectum, much higher for meat eaters, probably because of the higher levels of bile and fatty acids in the colon. Meat-based diets put too much iron in our bodies, especially *heme* iron, raising the risk of heart attack, a problem especially for men because women, until menopause, have a monthly purging of excess iron with menstruation. Some of the drugs given to treat various conditions more common among meat eaters (e.g., high blood pressure) can inhibit your sexual functioning.

The list goes on, but suffice it to say that meat eaters just plain have more health problems than those on plant-based diets, problems that can easily affect sexuality. Women suffer the same negative health affects of an animal-based diet as men do. Their exemption from conditions caused by excess iron disappears with menopause, which in our meat-and-dairy culture also brings such problems as hot flashes and night sweats, heart disease, and osteoporosis—all of which are much less common in cultures where soy products, rich in phytoestrogens, are the protein of choice or of economic necessity. Eating tofu and other soy products also seems to reduce the chances of breast cancer very significantly.

Now we start to get more specific. Excess free radical activity in the body is more common among omnivores than among vegetarians. Free radicals are damaged oxygen molecules, and, once damaged, they damage healthy cells. The results are a compromised immune system, premature aging, and an increased risk of cancer. There are two ways to deal with free radicals: prevent them from forming or counteract them after they've formed. A smart strategy uses both approaches. A diet rich in *antioxidants* like beta-carotene and vitamins A and E—found in vegetables and fruits, not animal foods—can help neutralize the effects of free radicals, while eliminating extracted oils (saturated and unsaturated, animal, fish, or even vegetable) and avoiding overdoses of iron, especially heme iron, can help limit free radical production.

But it gets a lot more specific than that, and most specific for men. It's discussed in a number of texts, including *Food for Life* by Neal Barnard, M.D., of the Physicians Committee for Responsible Medicine. One result of free radical activity is *atherosclerosis* the formation of plaques in the arteries, decreasing the interior diameter of the arterial walls. This restricts the flow of blood to the brain and heart, creating a tendency toward stroke and heart attack—for both men and women. As plaques form in the arteries of the legs, a painful condition develops that makes it difficult and awkward to walk. This is called *claudication*, a Latin word meaning "to limp." Ironically, it can also cause a man to *go* limp as well, because claudication also affects the arteries that supply blood to the penis. With sexual excitement, assuming arteries free of plaques, blood rushes to the penis, engorging it and making it erect. In our meat-eating culture, an astounding one-fourth of all men over age sixty are impotent. So you might say that to help keep "the animal in you" alive, you need to keep dead animals out of your body.

In his book, Dr. Barnard puts it a bit more gingerly but succinctly in explaining why people pay more attention when he talks about the sexual impact of dietary choices:

> *People do have trouble picturing their coronary arteries, while other parts of the male anatomy have a tremendous psychic presence.*

While men can certainly develop mutually satisfying sexual practices not dependent on a sustained erection, most would prefer this to be a matter of choice, not necessity, an expansion of repertoire rather than a limitation.

The vegetarian movement is spreading more rapidly among women than among men. Roughly equal proportions of adult women and men in the United States are vegetarian and vegan, but among vegeteens there's an estimated four times as many girls as boys; in England a full one-fourth of all young women in their late teens and early twenties are now vegetarian. But as the implications of eating meat and other animal products soaks into the resistant male psyche, we can expect to see a noticeable increase in "sexuality veganism" among both younger men who want to avoid the sexual muting many of their elders have experienced, and older men who want to recover some of their former vitality, which is apparently possible. Even if you've messed up your sex life with animal products, lack of exercise, and other unhealthy foods and habits, it may not be too late. Both claudication and coronary heart disease are reversible, so there's every reason to believe that, with exercise and a change of diet, what will clear up in the heart and in the legs will also clear up in that organ of pleasure *between* a man's legs.

8

Seed Beginnings

But for the sake of some little mouthful of flesh we deprive a soul of the sun and light, and of that proportion of life and time it had been born into the world to enjoy.

PLUTARCH[1]

The origins of vegetarianism are obscured in the mists of prehistory. Many cultures have stories akin to the Judeo-Christian "Garden of Eden" vision, a time when humans lived in harmony with all creatures, where the lamb lay down with the lion, and where people did not "hurt nor destroy in all God's holy mountain." Some take such stories literally, as referring to a golden age that our "sinfulness" has taken us away from. (The original biblical term translated as "sin" actually means "missing the mark.") Others interpret them as a desire to return to the innocent days when we were little babies, or even in our mother's protective womb. However it is viewed, it's a common vision in the hearts of people from a wide range of cultures.

Social movements, too, often describe their goal as a peaceful world—no more war, no hunger, no violence or exploitation—although in most such movements, this peaceful vision has been limited to our own kind (i.e., human beings). In any case, both religion and psychology show our deep-seated yearning for peace and harmony. When we do violence against others, human or otherwise, we also do psychological violence to ourselves. We become psychically numbed. We develop calluses on our souls.

All beings tremble before violence.
All fear death.
All love life.
See yourself in others.
Then whom can you hurt?
What harm can you do?

Buddha

Thou shalt not kill.
The Sixth Commandment, Exod. 20:13

While most religions talk about a peaceful vision, some encourage it more broadly than others. Most in their modern forms focus their concern almost exclusively on humans, but the sacredness of *all* life is fundamental to the ancient Eastern religions of Jainism and Zoroastrianism. Many sects of Hinduism today are strictly lacto-vegetarian, basing their diet in ancient scripture. When Buddhism, which originated as a reform movement within Hinduism, traveled to China, where milk was not widely used, it dropped milk products and became vegan, developing a wide variety of soy- and wheat-gluten-based "fake meats" to wean the carnivorous Chinese away from eating flesh. Huge community feasts were sponsored by Buddhist temples. Even today Chinese Buddhist clergy and some lay people are vegan (they'll say "vegetarian"), and it's considered an ideal even by those who don't practice it. The Essenes, Nazarenes, and early Christian Gnostics, among others, practiced vegetarianism. The Catholic Trappist monks are vegetarian, and the Seventh Day Adventists base their diet in biblical scripture:

> *And God said, behold,*
> *I have given you every herb bearing seed,*
> *which is upon the face of all the earth,*
> *and every tree, in the which is the fruit*
> *of a tree yielding seed;*
> *to you it shall be for meat.*
>
> GEN. 1:29

Actually, most Greek and Hebrew words translated in the Bible as "meat" didn't refer to animal flesh at all, but simply to food in general. This happened because in the time of King James, who authorized the translation of the Bible into English, the term "meat" meant "food" or "sustenance," not necessarily (and usually not) animal flesh. We still use terms like "nut meat," and when we talk of "the meat of the matter," it means the kernel, essence, or substance—not dead flesh.

akilah, maakal, okel, oklah = what is eaten, food
akal, barah = to eat
baruth, biryah = food, eating
brōma = food, meat
brōsimos = eatable, what may be eaten
brōsis = act of eating, food
lechem = bread, food, flesh
mazon = food
minchah = an offering, present
path = morsel
pathbag = morsel or portion of food

phāgo = to eat, feed on, consume, corrode
prosphagion = any thing to eat
tereph = torn food
trapeza = table
trōphe = nourishment
tsedah = hunting, venison, provision

The translation of all these terms into "meat" was accurate at the time of the King James translation, but because the meaning of the word "meat" has changed in the centuries since then, the translation is no longer accurate in the context of modern English. This has helped lead Christianity astray from a dietary application of the message of peace preached by its founder. Vegetarianism was common among early Christians, and Jesus may well have been vegetarian; the "loaves and fishes" story may have been symbolic rather than literal, since a fish was a secret sign used by early underground Christians sought out and persecuted by the state. In any case, it's hard to imagine Jesus, as Christians envisage him, working in a slaughterhouse or in a factory farm.

The attitude toward animals in Christianity is also influenced by another apparent mistranslation. The Old Testament states that "man" has a divinely granted "dominion" over animals. Biblical scholars tell us that a more accurate translation is "stewardship," not "dominion." Just as a good ruler should be kind and respectful to the citizens in his or her domain, so are we expected to act benevolently toward other-than-human animals under our power.

Learning how such translations are incorrect or no longer correct can help us come back to an understanding we have lost: that changing our hearts is intertwined with changing our diets, and that we can be defiled by what goes into our mouths as surely as by what comes out of them. If we idolatrously follow a printed or spoken word instead of our innermost wisdom, we can be led astray, as often happens in religions. At one point in its history, vegetarianism itself came to be demonized by religious authority.

> *The church so hated these good people, the Albigenses, a "heretical" Christian sect of thirteenth century France . . . that their vegetarian habits were not only represented as signs of a diabolical heresy, but were also used as a means to detect and convict them. For when prisoners were taken, sheep were led to them and knives provided for their butchery. Those who refused to kill the animals were burnt at the stake, and the majority did refuse since to take sentient life violated the very basis of their faith.*[2]

Considering the repression of nature, of human senses, and of spirit carried out in the name of the church, it's not surprising that a number of people are turning to modern reconstructions of ancient, pre-patriarchal religions that celebrate rather than denigrate nature and sensuality, and for whom the natural world and the body are sacred. One woman who grew up listening to her daddy preach from the pulpit every Sunday expressed this response in song:

> *Run from the churchyard, the word and the cross*
> *Run to the forest, the rivers and rocks*
> *You will find the green altar deep in the moss*[3]

People of this persuasion sometimes wear with pride the name applied with disdain or worse by Christians and others: "pagan." The word itself comes from the Latin, meaning simply "country dweller." With the spread of Christianity in Europe, it was the city people who converted first and, as city people often do, they looked down on people in the countryside and their beliefs and practices. The umbrella term "pagan" covers a broad diversity of beliefs. But "pagan" religions don't have exclusive claim to celebrating nature as divine—as the existence of groups like the Albigenses attests. That spirit is alive in modern Christianity, as denominational publications begin to reflect on the spiritual implications of the ecological reality we're being forced to face, giving rise to the awareness that we are part of the Earth, interdependent with all life, not above or apart from it—deep ecology on the religious level. In creation-centered spirituality the divine (God) is considered to be in everything, and everything in the divine.

With few exceptions, however—such as *some* Hindus, Jains, Buddhists, and pagans, quite a few Seventh Day Adventists, and a few other Christian sects—religions as we know them, including creation-centered, pantheist, or pagan ones, are not vegetarian. (Pagans persecuted early Christians just as Christians, once in power, persecuted pagans.) Still, in all major and minor religions and spiritual belief systems that I know of, there are parables or other teachings about caring for animals, the environment, and our own bodies; all it takes is a little moral imagination to make the leap into vegetarianism. Mohammed apparently ate little meat, and in Mecca, where he was born, no slaughter may take place; pilgrims approaching Mecca are not supposed to kill even insects.

Every political or religious belief system seems to have within it both the potential for freedom and celebration on the one hand, and on the other hand, narrow-mindedness, dogmatism, and oppression. Put another way, every religion, every culture, is like a storehouse full of more beliefs, practices, and customs than we could ever possibly use in our lives. Some are noble and beautiful, others violent and oppressive. Each of us has the inescapable responsibility to choose which of those things represent the best in us, and to apply them in our lives, leaving the rest behind. Even if we choose to unquestioningly follow some authority, we have *chosen* to do so.

Some ethical vegetarians manage to find a working relationship with their nonvegetarian religions, or become voices of conscience and of challenge, voices for change. Some form more sympathetic congregations or informal gatherings, while others wind up rejecting or drifting away from the traditions that don't seem to embrace their inner voice. Many Roman Catholics working for animal rights and welfare were shocked by the church's disavowal of their concerns in the new 1994 catechism.

The conflict between inner knowing and external authority is not new. When Gandhi was criticized for his attempts to liberate the lowest caste in India, the "untouchables," his opponents cited Vedic scripture in support of their position, much as my grandfather used the Bible to support his segregationist ideas. Gandhi replied to his critics:

> If the Vedas proclaim untouchability, I will brush aside
> the Vedas. There is no one untouchable in my eyes.
> Every human being is sacred.[4]

The late Isaac Bashevis Singer, himself a vegetarian, described this sort of conflict poignantly. In "The Slaughterer," we learn about pious and gentle Yoineh Meir, who had expected to become his town's rabbi but instead is offered, and pressured into accepting, the lucrative and prestigious job of ritual slaughterer. He balks at the idea of making his living by killing, but a rabbi counsels him that it would be presumptuous to try to be "more compassionate than the Almighty, the Source of all compassion."

So Yoineh Meir reluctantly accepts, only to find that what he does to the animals, he feels himself. Their terror at their approaching death, their cries and screams as they die at his hands, the spurting and splattering of blood, the skinning of animals not yet completely dead, the all-pervasive suffering and stench of the place come to haunt him more and more, day and night. Other people's bland acceptance of it all only adds alienation to his torment. Toward the end of the story, as the only way he can find out of his increasingly tortured state, out of the conflict between conscience and duty, he goes insane. As he does, he expresses a profound disillusionment (a casting off of illusions) that goes to the core of human liberation from social oppression:

> *"I'll have none of your favors, God! I am no longer afraid of your Judgment! I am a betrayer of Israel, a willful transgressor!" Yoineh Meir cried. "I have more compassion than God Almighty—more, more! He is a cruel God, a Man of War, a God of Vengeance. I will not serve Him. It is an abandoned world!" Yoineh Meir laughed, but tears ran down his cheeks in scalding drops.*
>
> *Yoineh Meir went to the pantry where he kept his knives, his whetstone, the circumcision knife. He gathered them all and dropped them into the pit of the outhouse. He knew that he was blaspheming, that he was desecrating the holy instruments, that he was mad, but he no longer wished to be sane.*[5]

Rejecting external authority in favor of one's inner truth is the starting point of the quest for sanity, for justice, for true spirituality, for personal and collective empowerment. To question authority is to move toward liberation; to live in reaction against it is to remain enslaved. If we can muster the courage to look honestly both at our tendency to unquestioningly accept authority and tradition and at our knee-jerk reactions against it, then we can begin to discover and move into the cleavage between these two forms of unmindfulness. From there, with an open heart and mind, we can start the process of inquiry and reevaluation essential to any life that seeks to be spiritual. From there also comes nonreactive action for positive personal change and cultural evolution.

And whether it's called spiritual or not, tapping into the river of joy that flows through all existence can be a vital counterbalance to the pain we become increasingly aware of. Some find meditation to be useful in this way. But Christopher Titmus, an internationally known meditation teacher who once ran for office as a local Green party candidate in the U.K. and some of whose students are social change (including animal rights) activists, has a note of caution about mediation. Though he feels it's important for spiritual health and growth, he warns against its "greatest danger"—getting swallowed up in our own internal experiences so much that we withdraw from the world and cease working for peace and justice and against ignorance and cruelty.

> *The entire world [is] comparable to a single organism,*
> *a body. . . . just as when the foot is in pain, the hand*
> *will spontaneously reach out to assuage the pain of*
> *the foot, in the same way—if you are no longer inhib-*
> *ited by self-centeredness—you will spontaneously*
> *reach out to assuage the pain of others.*[6]

There's so much that we don't know in this life, and we fill in the gaps—the gulfs—of our ignorance with faith and assumptions, intuition, and best guesses. When we do know something it's a shame not to act on it. We know that all creatures suffer more or less as we do, and that much, probably most, of the suffering we inflict on them is not at all necessary to our well-being—that meat kills, not just the animals, but us, too. With this awareness that goes beyond our own species, you may find yourself reading in a new light biblical passages counseling us to treat "others" as we ourselves would like to be treated—and few of us would want to be caged, separated from our families and friends, or killed.

Vegetarian footprints in the historical sand have been left by such advocates and practitioners of vegetarianism as Plato, Diogenes, Pythagoras, Plutarch, Porphyry, and

Plotinus; the Apostle Matthew and other early Christians; Shakespeare, Leonardo da Vinci, Isaac Newton, Rousseau, and Voltaire; Benjamin Franklin, Darwin, Wagner, Emerson, Thoreau, and Shelley; Susan B. Anthony, Gustav Mahler, Leo Tolstoy, Upton Sinclair, H.G. Wells, George Bernard Shaw, Albert Einstein, Thomas Merton, Albert Schweitzer, and Mahatma Gandhi. Cesar Chavez, founder of the United Farm Workers, was a vegetarian, as is the current president, Arturo Rodriguez. Member of Congress Andrew Jacobs and former California Supreme Court Chief Justice Rose Bird are vegetarian.

Other people walking in these footprints include Michael Jackson, Madonna, Paul McCartney, Patti Reagan Davis (the ex-president's daughter), Twiggy, Dick Gregory, William Shatner, Dennis Weaver, Chubby Checker, David Cassidy, Jimmy Cliff, Fred "Mister" Rogers, the late River Phoenix, and even former "Ronald McDonald" Geoffrey Giuliano. (See Appendix F: Vegetarian Celebrities for a more detailed list.)

The first vegetarian society in the Western world was formed in England in the mid 1800s, soon followed by one in the United States. In 1944 the world's first vegan society was established in England. World vegetarian congresses have been held in various countries, beginning with the first one in 1908, and there are now international vegan festivals every two years.

Sylvester Graham and John Kellogg were prominent U.S. vegetarians and health crusaders. These originators of Graham crackers and Kellogg cereals would roll over in their graves if they could see how their healthful whole grain products have been sugared, processed, and chemicalized beyond recognition.

While Graham and Kellogg have been criticized for being sex-negative zealots—Kellogg, for example, devised all sorts of bizarre and painful ways to discourage masturbation—they did make a valuable contribution to dietary reform. Vegetarianism by itself doesn't make us perfect in all or even most ways: Adolf Hitler was reportedly a vegetarian for health reasons. Remembering such wounded and flawed vegetarians can help us bear in mind our own wounds and blind spots, so that we can keep a little humility when dealing with the meat-eating society in which we live.

9

War and Peace

*From cutting the throat of a young calf to cutting the
throat of our brothers and sisters is but a step. While
we are ourselves the living graves of murdered animals,
how can we expect any ideal conditions on earth?*

ISADORA DUNCAN

Throughout history, peaceful ideals have existed side by
side with the reality of exploitation and violence. Astounding atrocities have been and continue to be committed
in the name of any number of causes that seemed noble to
their proponents, from national independence to national
unity, from propagating a religious "truth" to establishing
or defending a political ideology or creating an ideal society. Then there's tribal and racial separatism, and outright attempts to conquer, control, and exploit others. We
now have weapons so powerful they are making all-out
war obsolete by eliminating winners from the cruel game
of war.

Limited wars as in Bosnia or the Persian Gulf can be fought at a terrible price, but the world can't take sides and "go all the way" anymore. The demise of the Soviet Union has left the United States as the only remaining military superpower, but with the spread of nuclear materials and know-how, even "conventional" wars—over oil, for example—could quickly escalate to nuclear weapons. The same could happen if a more than usually immature or unbalanced person should become head of a nuclear state, something that even a superficial look at history tells us is likely to happen sooner or later, and probably sooner. And no Star Wars can defend against small, easily portable "suitcase nukes."

This same atomic century, interestingly enough, has also produced a rich history of alternative, nonviolent forms of defense and liberation. From Martin Luther King to Corazon Aquino's rise to power in the Philippines and the massive student-led Chinese uprising of 1989 in Tienanmen Square, nonviolent political action seems to be coming of age. The reformers in Czechoslovakia held out against the 1968 Russian invasion far longer, by all estimations, than they could have resisted with military means: Russian troops expecting to find a counterrevolutionary "enemy" found the people in the streets by the millions, blocking the tanks' advance and asking the soldiers why they were there. Taken up by people in the former Soviet-bloc countries, nonviolent action accomplished within weeks what decades of Western nuclear threat could not: a dismantling of the "iron curtain."

As with armed struggle, there is no guarantee of victory and no assurance that what replaces the old system will be any better, but scholars such as Dr. Gene Sharp of Harvard University are now studying nonviolent political struggle—its history, how it works, and its potential for a civilian-based alternative to military means of social defense.

Gandhi was one of the prime developers of modern active nonviolence, and perhaps the first to envision a nonviolent army for national defense. He also advocated and practiced vegetarianism as a fundamental part of his philosophy, regretting his inability to give up milk products. (Trying to ensure his milk was humanely produced, he took his milk goats with him everywhere, even when he went to visit the Queen of England, though what happened to the other members of the goats' families is another matter.) For Gandhi, there was a connection between nonviolence in politics and nonviolence in diet, between violence to fellow humans and violence to other creatures.

Among Gandhi's major influences in developing his philosophy and politics were the writings of two men, one in the United States and the other in Russia. Henry David Thoreau was a would-be vegetarian, while Leo Tolstoy proclaimed vegetarianism to be a precondition for all moral development and practiced what he preached. Both were radical pacifists and campaigners for social and economic justice. In these men, the United States and Russia have a source of nonviolence to draw on in both politics and diet, waiting for the time when the leaders and the people will be ready to listen.

It's not that you have to believe in nonviolent political action to become a vegetarian, nor vice versa; you don't. There's nothing to keep a vegetarian from being a soldier or military leader, and many notable nonviolent activists have been meat eaters. Rather, the promise of a nonviolent civilian-based defense is based on the greater practical effectiveness of such means in many situations of cultural and political conflict, not necessarily a philosophical commitment to nonviolence in all areas of life. Though he felt they were related, Gandhi distinguished the two in Sanskrit, with *ahimsa* being the traditional Hindu ideal of doing no harm, while he coined the term *satyagraha* (literally, "clinging to truth") to refer to the commitment to fight for what is right without harming one's opponent, as exemplified by, say, the civil rights movement in the American South.

As a young man, John Robbins was heir to the Baskin-Robbins ice cream empire, and was being groomed to take on the mantle of the vast family business. He walked away from it because of the commercialism and the way the dairy industry exploits cows, wrote *Diet for a New America,* and created the EarthSave Foundation to promote veganism for humane and ecological reasons. According to his research, if only 10 percent of meat-eating Americans became fully vegetarian, the oil savings—6.8 million barrels a day—would be enough for us to stop importing foreign oil altogether. This is because it takes fifty to seventy-five times as much fossil fuels to produce a pound of meat as a pound of, say, soybeans. It takes petroleum products to grow the feed crops; to make the pesticides; to harvest the crops and get them to the feedlots; to transport cattle to feedlots and later to slaughterhouses; to operate and wash down the slaughterhouses; and then to transport the meat to warehouses, stores, and the home, refrigerated all the way. (Refrigeration in general not only consumes large amounts of fossil fuels in generating electricity, but has also destroyed a significant portion of the protective ozone layer with its refrigerants, resulting in increasing rates of skin cancer worldwide.)

While people in India and China use a barrel of oil per person per year and those in Taiwan use eleven, each of us in the United States uses *thirty-three* barrels of oil per year. We import and depend on millions of barrels of foreign oil every day, which requires us to spend huge sums preparing for military intervention in the Persian Gulf or elsewhere—and at times to back up our preparations with lives of our soldiers and other people—to protect "our" oil as well as to prop up governments controlled by drug cartels or those that have terrible human rights records, all because they sell us oil or a provide us a supply route. In a day and age when military conflict over oil supplies could escalate into chemical, biological, or nuclear war, anything that can reduce our dependence is a positive step toward world peace. Oil wars, political exploitation, and ecological degradation (like the Exxon Valdez disaster) are inevitable consequences of our love affair with the automobile, our general energy wastefulness, and our attachment to animal products. The more oil and other resources we use, the more we have to be ready to fight, kill, and die for the privilege. We will also see later in this book how both chemical agriculture and modern methods of "factory farming" animals got their start from the most destructive war so far in human history.

Many people concerned with making a better world say they have time for only a few issues and prefer to focus on helping human victims of violence and oppression. One person can't do everything, and pointed concentration of efforts on one issue will often yield more results than energies scattered in a dozen different places. This is true for *active* solidarity. For example, I can't give what I call active solidarity—speaking, circulating petitions, going to meetings, writing letters, lobbying members of Congress, demonstrating—for each and every cause that's important to me. It's physically impossible. But I can show *passive* solidarity. I may choose to focus my active energies on, say, a particular environmental clean-up campaign, but that doesn't keep me from cleaning up my sexist or racist conditioning, my homophobia, or my cultural attachment to animal products. This involves not so much *doing* something as *stopping* doing things that cause violence, oppression, or destruction in other areas; it's a way at least not to undermine the efforts of those working actively on other issues.

As violence increasingly permeates our society, an increasing body of scientific evidence indicates that the mere presence of guns, even if only seen and not touched, tends to bring out aggression in people. We are being forced to reexamine what we've thought of as our constitutional "right to bear arms," which a reading of the Constitution and a review of court decisions reveals to be a reference to organized, democratically controlled state militias, not individuals or private armies. Groups like the National Rifle Association have taken the phrase "the right to bear arms" out of its constitutional context and distorted it into armed individualism, and we are now harvesting the fruit: guns in schools, drive-by shootings, and roving autonomous "armies."

We as a people are finally beginning to see the many faces of violence in our lives and the impacts of our political, personal, and dietary choices.

> *If you wish to know*
> *Why there are disasters*
> *Of armies and weapons in the world*
> *Listen to the piteous cries*
> *From the slaughterhouse at midnight.*[1]

We may not know, scientifically, the psychological, social, and spiritual ripple effects of the factory farms and slaughterhouses dotting our landscape, but we do know the effects of using more than our fair share of the resources, effects that have been known for centuries.

> *Socrates: "And there will be animals of many kinds, if people eat them?"*
> *Glaucon: "Certainly."*
> *Socrates: "And the country which was enough to support the original inhabitants will be too small now, and not enough?"*
> *Glaucon: "Quite true."*
> *Socrates: "Then a slice of our neighbors' land will be wanted by us for pasture and tillage, and they will*

want a slice of ours, if, like ourselves, they exceed the limit of necessity, and give themselves up to the unlimited accumulation of wealth?"

Glaucon: "That, Socrates, will be inevitable."

Socrates: "And so we shall go to war, Glaucon, shall we not?"

THE REPUBLIC, PLATO[2]

10

That Others May Live

The book *Diet for a Small Planet* was first published in 1971. It brought a large wave of converts into the vegetarian fold, and for a new reason. In it, author Frances Moore Lappé documented the great waste of the world's protein and food (caloric) energy supply that results from feeding human-edible crops to "food" animals.

An average piece of cropland used to produce food for direct human consumption feeds up to fourteen times more people than a similar piece used to grow crops that are first fed to animals, which are then killed and eaten by humans. Such waste is especially common in the United States, Europe, and in our agricultural supply colonies in Central America and elsewhere. Fully half of all harvested acreage in the U.S., representing an enormous amount of protein, is fed to livestock.

This figure includes 90 percent of all corn, barley, and oats (ranging from 8–14 percent protein), over 90 percent of our soybeans (34–40 percent protein), and a quarter of all milk products (3–33 percent protein). Almost half of all "harvested" fish (15–25 percent protein) is used as animal feed.

In addition, *Diet for a Small Planet* also made an argument for combining, in the same meal, plant foods of complementary amino acid patterns—combining a food high in one amino acid with another low in that particular amino acid, like beans with rice. (Amino acids are the "building blocks" of protein.) This belief, propagated by many vegetarian and nutrition books since then, is now widespread. It's also outdated, because to get such protein maximization you don't need to eat the beans at the same meal as the rice, but within sixteen or so hours of each other. Lappé herself in subsequent writings has revised her original claim. She now says that "most people eating healthy diets need not be concerned about combining proteins." If you're living on a subsistence diet, it would be very wise to maximize protein assimilation, as traditional cultures have done. But in affluent societies such as ours, as long as you eat a variety of whole, healthful foods, it's actually difficult *not* to get enough protein—though, as discussed in Chapter 4, "Protein Pressure," it's easy to get too much, with potentially serious health consequences.

Sixty million people around the world starve or die of hunger-related diseases each year. Theoretically, that many people could be fed with the grain saved if only 10 percent of meat eaters in the United States became vegetarian. In reality, of course, just because *we* don't eat it doesn't necessarily mean it gets to those who *do* need it— we have, after all, a profit-based economic system in which money talks and those without it are voiceless, powerless. The political will—including the will to create more egalitarian economic structures without sacrificing economic incentive—must be present for our vegetarian grain savings to be fairly shared with others. But even under our present system there is immediate benefit to others from our going vegetarian. By not buying meat and animal products, we are greatly decreasing our demand for grains, which means that the upward pressure on grain prices (and on the land to grow it) is eased, prices are lowered, and the grains as well as beans and other crops become more affordable to those with little money. With grain being grown less intensively, fewer chemicals are needed, water stays cleaner, and more land can be used for parks, recreational areas, nature reserves, and so on. In short, there is nothing but good to come from adopting a plant-based diet.

> *Successive generations of vegans have shown that we don't need to create a hell on earth for animals in order to live well ourselves.*
>
> THE VEGAN SOCIETY (U.K.)

Ozone depletion continues, a major culprit being the methane produced by our massive concentrations of cows, while there are many and increasingly startling indications that global warming is indeed occurring. If this is the case, coastal areas of the great continents will be put under water, while thousands of South Sea (and other) islands which are only a few feet above water now will be slowly flooded out of existence, ancient homelands destroyed. The world has no institutions for dealing adequately with hundreds of thousands or tens of millions of new "boat people," rendered homeless not by war but by unrestrained industrialism and energy-greedy, animal-based agriculture, as our war against animals and nature causes unanticipated human casualties. In a time when immigration is a hot political topic exploited by opportunistic politicians, it's sobering to realize the future massive population shifts that we're creating in part by our animal-based dietary choices now, and it's time to investigate how plant-based choices can help alleviate those pressures.

But we don't have to look beyond our national borders to see the terrible human cost extracted by our addiction to animal products. The single most dangerous job, in an industry with the highest turnover and injury rate, is slaughterhouse worker. Spending our dollars for plant-based instead of animal-based foods creates more safety and less danger for the workforce here at home who produce what we eat.

11

Eating the World

We are not facing *an environmental crisis. We* are *the environmental crisis.*

ANONYMOUS

Because of growing feed for cows, pigs, and chickens instead of food for people, *twenty times* more land is needed to support a meat eater than to support a vegan. But it doesn't stop there. Low-cost meat consumption in the rich countries is made possible by cattle-for-export operations in countries where people are already hungry. Large landowners, not the people who work the land, decide what to grow for the world market. Since we in the rich countries can pay more for meat and bananas than poor people there can pay for subsistence crops of rice, beans, and vegetables, what *we want* gets grown instead of what *they need*. The result is that our meat and luxury food addictions are bringing about human hunger and starvation, just as surely as Japanese taste preferences are threatening whole species of whales. It's easy for us to feel indignant about the callous Japanese as we send our contributions to organizations like Greenpeace, but harder to see the destructive effects of our own dietary choices. (A good deal of grain is also used to make alcoholic beverages.)

The intensively chemicalized agriculture used to grow the amount of crops necessary to feed "food" animals contributes to soil and water pollution, and our taste for animal foods depletes groundwater reserves. A typical mixed plant and animal food diet requires about 2,500 gallons of water per day to produce, compared with 300 gallons for a plant-based vegan diet. The water supply is polluted from the runoff of staggering amounts of urine and fecal matter from factory farms, feedlots, and slaughterhouses. About 20,000 pounds of manure is produced each year by *each* cow, and less than half of that gets used as fertilizer. Of all organic waste pollution in the U.S., 10 percent comes from humans, 90 percent from livestock.

What's true for "spaceship Earth" is more critically true for planned space colonies and long-term living aboard space stations. The National Aeronautics and Space Administration realizes that when space environments start producing food in controlled ecological life-support systems instead of transporting it from Earth at astronomical expense, animal products will be out of the question because they're such a wasteful use of the nutrients in plants. In 1994, NASA convened a workshop with experts on vegetarian and vegan diets—including Frank Salisbury, a plant physiologist at the University of Utah; Michael Klaper, M.D.; and Suzanne Havala of the Vegetarian Nutrition Practice Group of the American Dietetic Association—to discuss nutrition and food production in space. The information was well received, and resulted in a NASA technical report on the subject.

By shifting to a plant-based diet, we can use less land to produce more food with better human nutrition and much less reliance on chemical fertilizers and insecticides. Water and energy will be conserved, soil fertility restored, global warming slowed or reversed, and biological diversity nurtured instead of assaulted. Fewer endangered species will become extinct, since more and more farmland won't have to be carved out of virgin forests in order to grow crops for protein-wasting animal agriculture.

These forests, together with ocean phytoplankton, are the "lungs of the planet." They're also a cradle of biological strength and diversity for food crops and medicines worldwide, and are being rapidly depleted. Sixty acres of tropical forests are cut down every minute, primarily to satisfy our greed for meat. A *four-ounce* hamburger produced on cleared tropical rain forest land requires the destruction of *half a ton* of plant and animal life growing in an area the size of a small kitchen. With the cutting of forests, whole species disappear—about 1,000 per year in Central America alone. Deforestation is especially ominous for the larger animals who need very large areas to maintain minimum viable populations.

This "hamburger imperialism" has already destroyed nearly half of Central America's tropical rain forest to supply cheap meat for U.S. fast-food chains. When we eat meat, we are devouring the water, the land, people's quality of life, and the world itself.

A good deal of this destruction could be prevented through de-escalation of our industrial assault on nature coupled with a vegetarian orientation in development projects in the undernourished parts of the world. Widespread vegetarianism could help those who need it most to get more nutrition per dollar invested or per acre cultivated. As it is now, inequitable land distribution, credit manipulation by banking interests, and the drive for short-term private profits result in the large-scale production of luxury exports like bananas, coffee, recreational drugs, and meat, while the people go hungry. Children, weakened from malnourishment, die from such simple afflictions as diarrhea—about a million each year worldwide.

Those of us in the overdeveloped, overindustrialized, overconsuming, and overfed countries have a very unique and crucial role to play in restoring ecological balance and alleviating world hunger. When we spend our money on foods other than the animal products and luxury food imports that push the price of land and basic foods beyond the reach of the poor, we also help set positive trends.

Films, VCR technology, and satellite television are revolutionizing cultures and creating a world media culture promoting western values. Even poor, remote, third-world villages often have at least one television exposing the villagers to this emerging world media culture. Throughout history, poor folks have wanted to live like the rich. Today, this is translated to a global scale, with people in poor countries wanting to copy the overindustrialized countries in all sorts of ways, like diet and transportation. Americans are so well known the world over as big meat eaters that many people in other countries are surprised, sometimes amazed, to meet an American traveler who's vegetarian.

In China, which has a fifth of the planet's human population, the increased consumption of animal foods is causing the importation of so much grain that, if the trend isn't stopped and reversed soon, it will gobble up the whole world's grain supply, pushing the poor of the world into actual hunger, and those already hungry into their graves—or into war or revolution. Even if our hearts are hardened to starving people, our minds can still understand that having a lot of people desperate for food in the world is not in our best interests. Hungry and starving people will follow any pedagogue, any warmonger, who promises food. You and I would do the same in their situation.

Because it's simply impossible for the earth to support all humans at the consumption level that we in the wasteful West, and especially in the United States, are accustomed to, we have a great responsibility to stop setting such a bad example for the poor of the world to copy. Though the way we eat is only a part of the problem, an excellent place to start setting a better example is by getting animal products out of our diet. Our changes, because of the role of the United States in the world, have a "ripple" effect much greater than what we can see in our own personal lives.

The problem of world hunger is as political as it is agricultural and technical. The over-industrialized nations stand in a position of economic and military dominance over the rest of the world. Wouldn't it be better to encourage greater national and bioregional independence by assisting agricultural development along basically vegetarian, sustainable, mostly self-sufficient lines, rather than maintain dependency through ongoing, politically motivated food giveaways on the one hand, and meat and luxury food production and consumption on the other?

The last two decades has witnessed the growth of the diverse Green movement, centered around a commitment to meeting human needs with minimum damage to other life-forms and without compromising the ability of future generations to also meet their needs. When you think of it, it seems pretty basic, but it's something that has somehow escaped other ideologies and political parties.

A political expression of the Green movement is the Green Party (the two are carefully distinguished, with the Green movement being much bigger, and the Party being more focused), first in Europe and now in the United States and other countries. Green parties have qualified to be on the printed ballot—not just as write-ins—in California, Alaska, Hawaii, New Mexico, Arizona, Oregon, and probably

other states by the time you read this. These parties usually don't have a very big chance to win statewide office at
present, but participating in elections brings vital ecological
messages to the electorate and builds credibility for future
electoral contests. Greens tend to believe it's better to vote
for what you want and not get it (yet) than to vote for what
you don't want (the lesser of two evils) and get it. Still, they
try to balance idealism with political reality. In one
statewide election they chose not to field a gubernatorial
candidate in order not to draw votes from the mainstream
candidate who they saw as more "greenish"; instead, they
ran someone for lieutenant governor and focused their
campaign energies there.

Because our electoral system makes it almost impossible for third parties to have any influence, there is considerable interest in "proportional representation" among
Greens. Under proportional representation, any party that
gets, for example, 12 percent of the vote in elections for
Congress would get 12 percent of the congressional seats.
As it stands in the U.S., a party could get, say, 40 percent of
the votes in every single congressional district in the country and still get no seats in Congress because they didn't
"carry" any of the districts. Many democracies have some
form of proportional representation.

The Greens are not a vegetarian movement per se, and
members and supporters include some avid hunters. But
you'll find far more vegetarians and vegans in the Greens
than in any other major or minor political party in the
country, or any other movement except the vegetarian,
vegan, and animal rights movements themselves. The
platform of the California Green Party, for example, not
only commits to outlawing factory farming but says: "In
the interests of the environment, health, and nonviolence,
we encourage individuals to adopt a vegetarian . . .
or . . . vegan lifestyle." While the term "lifestyle" is an
overly broad term when talking about diet, the inclusion of

such wording in any statewide party's platform is a definite, hopeful sign of the times. Articles on vegetarianism, veganism, and animal rights appear from time to time in Green publications.

The Greens are perhaps the only current social/political movement in which you can find serious challenges to the "growth god" that the modern world worships—the idea that economic growth is inherently good. Our economy is based on the assumption that economic growth should and can continue indefinitely. Yet the United States, with a very small proportion of global population, already consumes the lion's share of the world's limited and dwindling natural resources. That means that each of us consumes, directly and indirectly, far more resources than a person in another country. At a "modest" real growth rate of 3 percent, a city's, a nation's, or a planet's consumption of resources will *double* every twenty-four years.[1] The resource base and the ecosystem itself are simply not able to support such growth indefinitely, especially not for all the world's people. An economic policy or system based on continued growth not only destroys natural systems, but heightens competition for limited resources and thereby increases the chances for catastrophic resource wars.

Class conflict has been avoided by liberals and conservatives alike by relying on continued economic growth. If both the rich and the poor get "better off" (consuming at higher levels) over time, everybody will be more or less happy. But, though we don't always know what they are or when the crunch will come, there *are* natural limits; the only question is not *whether* we bring our cancerous economic growth under control, but *when* and *how*, voluntarily or as a result of an economic or ecological collapse. As we're increasingly forced to accept natural ecological limits to growth and as our economic system sputters and falters in its attempts to produce continuous growth, we are having to confront things we have preferred to sidestep, namely, how our economic and political system distributes goods and services, and what our *real* needs are.

Our needs for food, shelter, and clothing can be satisfied by production of economic goods. Beyond this, though, our needs are not primarily economic, but noneconomic "things" such as safety, touch, love, and community.

We tend to throw the term "community" around rather loosely, talking about "the medical community," "the gay community," or "the vegetarian community." But real communities are not categories of profession, sexual preference, or diet. They are the ground in which various forms of families can take root, and in which our individuality can flower, as distinct from our individual-*ism*, which reinforces our view of ourselves as separate, isolated egos, just as families not rooted in community are separate, isolated, vulnerable, stressful, and often unfulfilling.

The economic forces that propel us apart, scattering us far and wide, are reinforced by our housing patterns. If our housing had been deliberately designed to keep us separated, it would result in pretty much what we've got, especially in suburbia: separate houses that we can actually drive into without any contact with neighbors, and with no neighborhood stores, no Laundromats, no community. City dwellers, too, can live for years without knowing the people a few apartment doors away.

This is in sharp contrast to cohousing, conceived and developed in northern Europe as multiage communities combining the best of two worlds—privacy and shared living—without ideologies or gurus. Each family or single individual has their own private, self-contained dwelling, but houses (or apartments) are arranged so that each person comes into contact with others in the course of everyday coming and going. Decisions are democratically made, usually by consensus, and there's a common house (or, for apartments, a large common room) for shared activities, including, usually, optionally shared evening meals a few times a week. Sharing some characteristics with cohousing are "eco-village" developments or transformations of old neighborhoods into real, safe communities. The movement toward sustainable, community-engendering forms of housing like cohousing and eco-villages are ways to find sufficient privacy within the context of community, rather than sacrificing the latter to the former. (See Appendix C: Organizations.)

Undermining community distorts our individuality into individualism; it keeps us in denial of how interconnected we are and of how our individual actions impact on others. An industrialist feels the "right" to dump waste onto "his" land; a landowner assumes the "right" to cut down all the trees on "her" land. We strive to maximize profit, pay, convenience, or personal security without regard to the consequences for others. There's a story from the Talmud about two people adrift in a wooden boat. When one starts drilling a hole in the bottom of the boat, the other gets upset and tells him to stop. "What business is it of yours?" says the driller. "I'm only drilling under *my* seat."

We in the overindustrialized West have more gadgets than any people in history, but often less of what would satisfy us on deeper levels. There's little money to be made selling self-esteem or helping people develop personal intimacy or community, and people who feel good about themselves and are interconnected with each other are harder to exploit. But there's plenty of money to be made on selling products with the false promise that they'll make up for our emotional, social, spiritual, or kinesthetic impoverishment.

Another part of the Green vision is the idea of sustainable agriculture that doesn't destroy the soil, that doesn't pollute the water, that doesn't foul the air, and that doesn't bring disease and death to farmworkers, consumers, and animals.

A healthy topsoil is the basis for any viable society. Topsoil depletion has been the cause of the decline of many great civilizations, and ours is doing in a few hundred years what's taken others thousands of years. In the short time since Europeans first came to this continent, we've lost three-quarters of our topsoil. We would still have an estimated 85 percent of that lost topsoil if it weren't for the raising of livestock. A vegan or vegetarian diet is a vital step toward saving the topsoil and ensuring that our children, and theirs, have enough to eat.

It's in the tradition of some Native American nations to ask how a decision will affect the next seven generations. From this perspective, there's no choice in the modern world but a plant-based diet, and it can't be reduced to a liberal–conservative, left–right issue. Though Greens tend to be associated somewhat with the left of the political spectrum (in the U.S., what we consider "left" would in many countries be considered middle-of-the-road or even conservative), it's not that simple. One of the slogans of the Greens has been "neither right nor left, but ahead," and Green analysis sharply critiques traditional liberal acceptance of chemical agriculture and constant-growth economics.

Liberals are more likely than conservatives to be vegetarian, but one out of twenty self-declared conservatives in the country is a vegetarian. If we take a look at the root of the word "conservative," we see "conserve." A vegetarian way of eating is an integral part of any true conservatism; it conserves natural resources, and in the process shores up national resource and energy independence. And no political camp has a monopoly on either compassion or cruelty, despite what members of opposing camps might wish us to believe.

Rachel Carson, in her seminal work *Silent Spring,* wrote:

As cruel a weapon as the cave man's club, the chemical barrage has been hurled against the fabric of life.

Chemical agriculture got its real start from the defoliants, nerve gases, and other chemical warfare agents developed during World War II. After the war, chemical companies found in farmers a new market for their deadly products humans. Government farm agents pushed these crop drugs heavily, industry refined them, and farmers experienced short-run crop increases using them. But agricultural poisons can also kill insects' natural predators and the little creatures in the soil that keep it healthy; over time, the target insects develop resistance to the poisons and soil quality deteriorates. The production gain proves short-lived, but by the time most farmers realize it, they are "hooked" as surely as a tobacco or heroin addict is hooked. Their dependence on a regular chemical fix makes it hard for them to go back to traditional organic methods. A number of large corporate farms, in fact, are actually owned by chemical companies who rake in the money with both hands.

Five pounds of pesticides are used per person per year in U.S. agriculture. Chemically grown foods retain traces of the poisons used in growing, and these poisons get concentrated in animal flesh and products. The poisons are especially bad for the farmworkers, and for the communities surrounded by agricultural land. These people get much heavier exposure than consumers do; children and the unborn are most vulnerable to chemicals that cause "toxic womb" diseases and birth defects. Even for adults, these chemicals can bring sickness and death. The United Farm Workers' boycott of nonorganic table grapes is an attempt to force growers to stop using the most deadly pesticides, which are used only to keep the grapes cosmetically unblemished.

The chemical toll continues. Toxic runoff from chemical farming is a major source of water pollution, soils are depleted and given chemical fixes instead of developing their fertility, and staggering numbers of birds and mammals wander into poisoned fields and die.

Increasingly, though, farmers are going against government and chemical industry advice and are learning to "Just Say No" to their chemical addiction, making the switch to organic farming. Others are weaning themselves more gradually from agricultural chemicals with integrated pest management (IPM)—the use of primarily organic methods, with chemical pesticides as a backup in case of an insect invasion. Whether in farming, sex, diet, or life in general, the ability to say a firm, clear "No" to things that are bad for us opens the way for saying "Yes" to positive developments that would otherwise not have been possible.

Organically grown produce is not available in most stores, but it can be found by searching for farmers' markets, co-ops, and natural food stores, or by contacting small farmers directly. By placing an ad in your local paper, you may be able to locate farmers who use organic or mostly organic methods or integrated pest management. Such an ad can also help you find people to form an organic buying club. Community Supported Agriculture (CSA) is an arrangement between local organic farmers and consumers that satisfies not only the need for good natural food but also for some sort of personal relationship between farmers and consumers. There is a national toll-free number that connects interested consumers with producers in their areas (see Appendix C: Organizations).

If you don't know the farmer, how can you know that produce that's claimed to be organic actually is? How do you know that if it was organically grown, it wasn't treated with chemicals when shipped? The key word here is *certified*. Various states have passed laws defining "organic," and there are organic producers' organizations which certify that produce was organically grown. Congress passed the Federal Organic Foods Production Act to establish national definitions and guidelines, to test foods for contamination, to certify growers, and to inspect imported organic produce. It is scheduled to go into effect in 1996 (see Appendix E: Mail-Order Food and Sustainable Agriculture).

Opposed to wasteful, deadly chemical (and now nuclear, with food irradiation) agriculture, organic farming is a real step in the right direction, and one well worth supporting. Still, as it's now done, it's part and parcel of our animal-based agriculture system, using large amounts of animal manure from factory farms; blood- and bonemeal from slaughterhouses; and fishmeal from billions of fish and sea creatures dredged from their watery homes, killed, dried, and ground up into fertilizer.

Organic agriculture doesn't claim to be humane, but it does claim to be ecological. If you look only at the product and the health of the soil it's grown on, present organic practices are fantastic. But if you step back and take a more comprehensive, holistic view, if you look at where the animal inputs come from and the ecological impact of their production, then animal-based organic methods start to look considerably less ecological than at first glance. (Improperly processed animal wastes used as fertilizers can also pass animal diseases to human consumers of the produce.)

A few farmers use only or mostly "green manures" and "stockless rotations," but it's difficult to locate them because the old patchwork of organizations certifying and encouraging organic farming either do not distinguish between animal and plant inputs, or will not divulge that information because of confidentiality constraints.

Research in veganic farming—using no animal input except that from the over four *tons* of critters living in each acre of healthy organic soil—is still in the initial stages, unsupported by government or foundation grants. Quite a few people garden veganically and there's even a how-to book about it, but there are only a very few farms in the world that call themselves "veganic," and only one in the U.S. The attachment to the use of animal manures by some organic advocates parallels the overall society's attachment to animal foods, but there are individuals in the field who are interested in moving away from animal manures and toward plant-based fertilization. With the National Organic Program's new national organic standards and a single certifying agency (see Appendix E: Mail-Order Food and Sustainable Agriculture), there is a single place to focus concerns about customers' rights to know whether food is produced with animal or veganic inputs and methods.

Until veganically grown products become available, we make our food choices out here in the real world, doing the best we can. As the current group of vegetarian and vegan youth matures, making their wants known to the natural food stores where they shop, and as others express concern over personal and planetary health and come increasingly to understand the ecological importance of unplugging from all aspects of animal agriculture, a market for veganically grown produce will begin to open up, waiting for enterprising farmers to get the jump on their competition by switching to veganic methods. Such farmers will be able to tap into a vegetarian and vegan market growing nationwide and even internationally.

Our cars, manufacturing processes, and energy-intensive animal agriculture will reportedly suck most of our domestic oil wells dry within a couple of decades, giving a greater urgency to Earth Day than it had at its inception. Celebrated every April, it has become an institutionalized event across the country. Critics note that it's often sponsored by businesses and corporations that are more part of the problem than part of the solution, its message having been diluted into issues that do not challenge lifestyle, diet, or business practices in any fundamental way. But its ecological importance is being resurrected by vegetarian and vegan activists who have begun to protest against and challenge some of its corporate sponsors, and to use the occasion as a forum to edu-

cate the public about the ecological importance of assign-
ing animal agriculture to its overdue place in the dustbin of
history.

*If the earth were only a few feet in diameter, floating
a few feet above a field somewhere, people would
come from everywhere to marvel at it. People would
walk around it, marveling at its big pools of water, its
little pools, and the water flowing between the pools.
People would marvel at the bumps on it, and the
holes in it, and they would marvel at the very thin
layer of gas surrounding it and the water suspended
in gas. The people would marvel at all the creatures
walking around the surface of the ball and at the
creatures in the water. People would declare it precious because it was the only one and they would
protect it so that it would not be hurt. The ball would
be the greatest wonder known, and the people would
come to behold it and be healed, to gain knowledge,
to know beauty, and to wonder how it could be.
People would love it and defend it with their lives,
their own roundness could be nothing without it. If
the Earth were only a few feet in diameter.*[2]

12

Blood on the Tongue

A carnivorous diet not only decimates tropical rain forests, snatches food from hungry mouths, and pushes us closer to ecological catastrophe, it also causes immense suffering for the animals involved. Children are able to understand easily the wrongness of killing animals, which is why misguided parents hide the gory realities of animal agriculture from them, and why the meat, milk, and egg industries provide slick "educational" materials for schools, showing smiling animals being "processed" into meat-counter delicacies. In the U.S. alone, almost 5 *billion* animals are killed each year for humans to eat, and they don't go meekly—they try to get away from the knives and the clubs and the guns, just like you or I would. Milk cows and egg-laying chickens are not exempt; they're sent to slaughter as soon as their overworked, stress-wracked, chemically overstimulated bodies prematurely wear out, causing their production to go down.

*The modern layer is, after all, only a very efficient con-
verting machine, changing the raw material (feed-
stuffs) into the finished product (the egg)—less, of
course, maintenance requirements.*[1]

FARMER AND STOCKBREEDER

In the egg industry, newly hatched male chicks, lacking
the desired taste and texture of the specially bred "broilers"
and unable to lay eggs, are culled into heaps or bags of
discarded, suffocating bodies to be ground into pet food or
fertilizer. Sometimes they're tossed alive into the grinding
machine. If they're lucky, they're gassed to death.

In the broiler units, on the other hand, it's the female
chicks who are discarded. Both "broilers" and "layers" are
traumatically "debeaked" with hot mini-guillotines, without
anesthesia. This is done to minimize the mutual mutilation
that they otherwise inflict on each other, a result of having
their natural social order and biological needs frustrated:
They're "housed" in wire cages for life with no room even
to spread their wings; up to twelve birds may be packed
into a four-square-foot cage. Such "prison eggs" have been
banned in some places in Europe, and debeaking has been
outlawed in Holland and Denmark. Sweden has banned all
factory farming altogether. Meanwhile, debeaking and
other abuses remain completely legal in the United States,
despite the illusion created by brand names referring to
"happy" hens or "natural" eggs.

Under such conditions, even though debeaked, many
birds peck each other severely, while some starve only
inches away from food and water, their wings or feet
caught in the cages' wire mesh. Chickens are viewed as
being too cheap to justify close supervision, much less veterinary care; with automated feeding and waste removal
(and, for layers, egg collection), their only human contact
may be the daily visit of the overseer, who enters only to

remove the dead. Tens of thousands of birds may be kept under one roof. Crowding, stress, and heavy drugging against profit-threatening epidemics take their toll. Layers, who under more natural conditions would live fifteen or twenty years, are "spent hens" (an industry term) within a year and a half.

At career's end, they are then crammed into even more crowded cages for the ordeal of transport that we witness on our highways; many die en route. At their destination, the survivors are hung by their feet upside down on a conveyer belt that pulls them through an electric stunning chamber into the killing room. There, a constantly whirring buzz-saw rips into their jugulars, except for the unlucky ones who are still conscious. They sometimes jerk away from the blade at the last moment, and get dropped alive into the scalding defeathering water.

The products of this process are neatly Saran wrapped for display in supermarket meat counters, and uniformly arranged for our convenience in packages of six, twelve, or eighteen. Turkeys suffer a fate similar to that of chickens, including being given growth hormones and other drugs to artificially increase their size and weight so the factory farmers can make more money and keep up with the competition.

In 1995, an animal rights activist in England offered $15,000 to any factory farmer who would stay for two weeks in a cage proportional to the size of a cage that a hen in intensive egg production lives in her whole life. Several tried, but none made it beyond a few days. Later in the same year, People for the Ethical Treatment of Animals began similarly challenging meat industry executives in various states in the U.S.

"Free range" or "cage free" eggs are now available in natural food stores, and the producers crow about it in their advertising and on their packaging. Unfortunately, these terms can be misleadingly used to mean the birds get only enough room to walk around a bit or even that they have a bigger than usual cage. However, some free range producers do give the birds quite a bit more room. Organic chickens are not raised as cruelly, because the business doesn't have recourse to drugs to combat epidemics in crowded conditions.

Still, as far as I know, no chickens other than pets are allowed to have a natural sex life, stay with their families, and live out their natural life spans. If you want to check out a particular egg producer for yourself, you can write them, asking them the following questions: Are your chickens caged or free roaming? What percentage of their time do they spend caged versus outdoors? How many square feet does each bird have? Are eggs gathered by hand, or is collection automated? How many birds do you have in your operation? Are they given any drugs in their feed orally, by injection, or in any other way? If so, what, and how? What percent of your eggs are fertilized? What do you do with the male and female chicks from these eggs? How long do you keep your birds, on average? Do you have a problem with birds injuring each other or themselves? If so, how do you solve the problem? Do you debeak? When you get rid of them, how do you do that, or who do you sell them to? What percentage of your birds die before sale or slaughter? How old are they when they're sold or killed? What percentage must be killed or sold because of injuries?

Forget the pig is an animal. Treat him just like a machine in a factory. Schedule treatments like you would lubrication. Breeding season like the first step in an assembly line. And marketing like the delivery of finished goods.[2]

HOG FARM MANAGEMENT

> *The breeding sow should be thought of, and treated as, a valuable piece of machinery whose function is to pump out baby pigs like a sausage machine.*[3]
>
> NATIONAL HOG FARMER

Pigs, sociable animals with one of the highest measured human-correlated IQs in the animal world, fare little if any better. In modern factory farms, they are often bred in "rape racks," stalls which hold the females immobile, allowing aggressive males sexual access at will. They live their lives in small stalls and on concrete or slatted floors. As with chickens, the ammonia stench from their accumulating urine and feces is a major cause of disease for the animals, especially respiratory disease, which even heavy drugging cannot prevent. Like other farm animals, they are increasingly being fed their own excrement mixed in with their feed.

Under intensive confinement, pigs engage in tail biting, which can progress, if unchecked, to cannibalism. Following the lead of poultry debeakers and cattle dehorners, pork industry "herdsmen" solve the problem quickly and efficiently by cutting off the pigs' tails without the bother and expense of anesthesia. This is far cheaper and easier than keeping them in more spacious cages or outdoors. At the slaughterhouse end of the pork production line, many pigs, their bodies and spirits weakened by constant and repeated abuse, simply give up and die before they get to the killing floor. Pork producers fret over this profit-threatening Porcine Stress Syndrome (PSS), but they're locked into capital-intensive production methods with its depersonalization of the animals in their charge.

Sometimes, however, even farmers hardened to the harsh realities of traditional animal "husbandry" and slaughter find they just can't take factory farm abuse anymore. One pig farmer angrily lashed out at an animal rights activist, saying: "It's hard enough to make a living these days without having to be concerned about all this [animal rights] stuff!" Later, he apologized, with tears in his eyes:

> *I'm sorry I got so mad at you before. It's not your*
> *fault. You are just showing me what I already know,*
> *but try not to think about. It just tears me up, some of*
> *the things we are doing to these animals. These pigs*
> *never hurt anybody, but we treat them like, like, like I*
> *don't know what. Nothing in the world deserves this*
> *kind of treatment. It's a shame. It's a crying shame. I*
> *just don't know what else to do.*[4]

If a farmer tries to actually act on such humane instincts in the world of agribusiness, he or she winds up at a sharp disadvantage in the marketplace. Slave-ship economics prevail—the more animals a farmer crowds into expensive buildings, the cheaper the overhead per animal, and the cheaper the meat. Even relatively humane producers simply can't compete economically.

Milk cows are also confined, and their male offspring are placed for life in tiny "veal crates" where they can barely move and can't turn around. Prevented from exercising, fed a deliberately iron-deficient diet, and kept away from sunlight, these calves' meat stays soft, tender, and white, producing the gourmet veal that some humans are conditioned to like so much, and at a price considerably less than that of "drop veal" from calves slaughtered immediately at birth. The mothers' udders are enlarged with drugs and selective breeding to the point that many can hardly walk; an udder may weigh over a hundred pounds. Kept constantly pregnant and full of drugs and overmilked, these mothers fare little better than their male offspring. Milk cows who would normally live twenty to twenty-five years are lucky to see their fourth birthday before, worn out, they're sent to slaughter.

You can buy organic milk in natural food stores. Depending on the company, the cows that produce this milk are probably treated better than (or not as bad as) cows raised nonorganically, if for no other reason than that without massive doses of drugs to prevent the spread of disease, they can't be kept as closely confined. Some of them actually have pasture to graze in. Still, they have their babies taken from them so humans can take the milk; the mother-child bond between a cow and her calf is intense, and both cow and calf will typically wail piteously for each other when separated. The calf, if male, will probably be sent to a veal production unit; he'll be desperate to suck his mother's teat, but be unable to. The female calves are put into milk production like their mothers. Even cows raised organically are kept repeatedly pregnant by artificial insemination (the semen inserted deep by a farmer's hand and arm) to keep the milk supply flowing, and when their production goes down or medical (veterinary) costs go up, they're sent to slaughter.

I don't know of a single dairy for which this isn't true; if you for some reason think you've found an exception, please write them and ask these questions: What percentage of waking time do your milk cows spend together in a pasture, in a fenced-in lot, or indoors, versus in isolated stalls? Are they milked by hand or by machine? Are they given any drugs in their feed, orally, by injection, or in any other way? If so, what, and how? What happens to the male and female calves of your milk cows? How long are male and female newborns allowed to be with their mothers before being taken away? How long do you keep your cows? When you get rid of them, how do you do that, or who do you sell them to? What percentage of your cows are killed or sold because of injuries or disease?

If the dairy owner or operator is forthright in her response, you may be unpleasantly surprised at some of the answers, but at least you've checked it out for yourself. Just keep a copy of your letter, and notice which of your questions they ignore.

Milk would be prohibitively expensive if it were produced by treating the cows well; by keeping old, no longer productive cows alive, providing them food, shelter, and medical (veterinary) care; and by refusing to sell their offspring into milk and veal production.

The switch toward intensive confinement, also called factory farming, was a spin-off from World War II, when, after the war, surplus military buildings were put to "good" use in chicken production. (So, like chemical agriculture, factory farming has its roots in the most destructive war so far in human history.) Overall, almost all U.S. eggs, 90 percent of the chicken meat, half of the pork and milk, and over 99 percent of the veal are now produced under varying degrees of intensive confinement.

There are few (and largely unenforceable) laws to protect so-called "food" animals the way, say, dogs and cats are at least theoretically protected from abuse by their owners. There is no effective legal deterrent to prevent an auctioneer, trucker, or slaughterhouse worker from beating, kicking, whipping, electric shocking, or otherwise abusing an animal who, for example, resists her offspring being taken away, prefers not to proceed to the killing floor, or inconsiderately breaks a leg when getting off a truck. (A few states have now passed laws requiring the killing of such "downed" animals, instead of leaving them to die of cold, heat, hunger, thirst, or their injuries.) In fact, food animals—like laboratory animals during experimental procedures—are specifically *exempt* from the provisions of the so-called Animal Welfare Act. This law stipulates, for example, that caged birds must be able to completely spread their wings—*except poultry.*

13

The Vegan Alternative

Never again may blood of bird or beast
Stain with its venomous stream a human feast
To the pure skies in accusation steaming
      PERCY BYSSHE SHELLEY, "REVOLT OF ISLAM"

Most people are unaware of the conditions under which most animal products are produced and of the suffering of the animals. They think, or hope, that their breakfast omelets and summer ice cream come from contented animals.

Even more than the actual killing, the factory farming system is a persuasive argument for veganism. While it's possible for a vegetarian living in the countryside to obtain milk and eggs humanely, this is rare. It's expensive to treat the animals well, keep their families together, allow them their natural social groupings, let them live out their natural lives even after milk and egg production have fallen off, and let the male calves and chicks live even though they don't produce milk or eggs. For former Beatle Paul

McCartney, reputedly the richest person in show business, this is no problem. He and his wife can easily afford to keep chickens and sheep on their farm, using the eggs and wool but not killing the animals.

Under modern economic and agricultural conditions, however, humanely produced milk and eggs are available only to a privileged few. Most of us—the mass of humanity—have only two choices: outgrow the taste for animal products or continue to participate in the ruthlessly efficient cruelties of animal agriculture. Unlike lacto- or lacto-ovo-vegetarianism, veganism is both cruelty-free *and* truly democratic. It's a diet that almost everyone—rich or poor, city or country dweller—can follow for their own betterment and for that of other humans, other creatures, and the earth. It's the only diet that is not only healthful and ecological, but also humane and consistent with the principle of social justice: that what we have, everyone should be able to have.

Henry David Thoreau wrote in his classic essay "Civil Disobedience":

> It is not a man's duty, as a matter of course, to devote himself to the eradication of any, even the most enormous, wrong; he may still properly have other concerns to engage him; but it is his duty, at least, to wash his hands of it, and, if he gives it thought no longer, not to give it practically his support.

To adopt a vegan diet is to withdraw our support from animal abuse, as we apply to modern realities the same principles that in a more pastoral age led humane people to embrace lacto-ovo-vegetarianism. An ongoing boycott of cruelty is an effective way to wash one's hands of the enormous wrongs done to nonhuman animals, to say "yes" to the concerns of the animal rights movement, and to affirm the best in ourselves. The inconvenience of reconditioning our taste buds is minor compared to the suffering we thereby relieve, and we are compensated with a clearer conscience and better health as we get all the protein, carbohydrates, and other nutrients we need, but without the fat and cholesterol that we'd get in a meat or vegetarian diet. Studies suggest that going vegan can reduce your chances of suffering from, or alleviate the symptoms of, the following:[1]

- Heart disease
- Breast cancer
- Prostate cancer
- Colon cancer
- Bowel cancer
- Indigestion
- Diabetes
- Eczema
- Arthritis
- Asthma
- Bronchitis
- Migraine
- High blood pressure
- Appendicitis
- Osteoporosis
- High cholesterol level
- Gall stones
- Kidney stones
- Constipation
- Food poisoning
- Irritable bowel syndrome
- Gastrointestinal bleeding

- Varicose veins
- Hemorrhoids
- Ulcerative colitis
- Mucus problems
- Salmonella
- Acne
- Chronic fatigue
- Allergies
- Muscle cramps
- Obesity
- Lactose intolerance
- Insomnia
- Thrombocytopenia
- Headaches
- Human "Mad Cow Disease" (if it proves contagious to humans)

One of the researchers in the massive China Diet and Health Study put it this way: "Our study suggests that the closer one approaches a total plant food diet, the greater the health benefit."[2]

Perhaps out of original necessity but now only out of habit and greed, we have institutionalized egg stealing and raised it to the *nth* degree. A lot of animals kill and eat other animals, but we're the only animal to drink the breast milk of another species. Many of us are never weaned, but nurse from cradle to grave, merely switching to the teat of a different, enslaved species at an early age. From this perspective, veganism is simply a part of growing up.

There's an idea floating around that veganism, and vegetarianism in general, is a white, middle-class thing, but a plant-based diet benefits lower-income folks at least as much as it does the well-heeled. I once had a college economics teacher who said that "Money may not buy happiness, but with it you can choose the kind of misery you live in." That's what we do when we use increased incomes to buy animal products, except that we also create misery for others in the process. The health problems that result hit all social classes alike, but lower income people are least able to afford medical care, days off from work because of illness, or a financial cushion for a disease-wracked old age. Unfortunately, the false association of vegetarianism and veganism with the well-heeled probably keeps a lot more poor people from getting on the bandwagon.

There are vegetarian traditions and trends in various segments of our society. Some cultures from Asia have a vegetarian tradition, and African-American comedian, social activist, and businessman Dick Gregory, himself vegan, has been preaching vegetarianism for decades. A 1994 Roper poll commissioned by the Vegetarian Resource Group showed no significant differences between the proportion of vegetarians and vegans among African-Americans and in the population at large. (Women and men were also equally likely to be vegetarian and vegan.) While this might come as a surprise to a lot of white people, it wouldn't surprise the ten students at a black college in Georgia who started a vegan raw foods restaurant, Delights of the Garden, that became so popular that it expanded to Washington, DC. Everyone of any color, language, or culture, rich or poor, can reap the benefits of a plant-based diet in better health and a clearer conscience, things that money simply can't buy.

Veganism is the second wave of the modern vegetarian movement, surging through the culture; led by the youth, it has yet to crest. The mushrooming of book (including cookbook) titles on vegetarianism is being followed by an increasing number of vegan ones. The term "vegan itself," practically unknown just a few years ago, has rapidly become part of our vocabulary. As health and ecological problems force us in the direction of a plant-based diet, and as our conscience awakens, veganism becomes the leading edge and lacto-ovovegetarianism retreats from that position, shifting toward the middle of the dietary spectrum. A barometer of this shift in the dietary spectrum is Weight Watchers: they instituted both vegetarian and vegan meal plans in the early 1990s and expanded them in 1995.

International Vegan Festivals are held every two years; in 1995 it was in the United States, in San Diego. Vegans International (VI) has coordinators in many countries, with new ones being added every few months (see Appendix C: Organizations). The country coordinators distribute (and, where necessary, translate) the VI newsletter. *Vegan Guides* for travelers in various cities have been written for Amsterdam, Berlin, London, Munich, New York, Paris, and probably other cities by the time you read this. There's even a book on how to write such a guide. Anyone with a computer and a modem can tap into global vegan resources, including an Internet "mailing list" called Vegan L. Though they often get it wrong, most airlines now include vegan meals as one of the options they offer, and when they do get it wrong, you can sometimes get some financial compensation. They usually call vegan meals "pure" or "strict" vegetarian, so you need to ask for definitions of the terms.

When two unemployed vegans who had been part of an informational leafleting of a McDonalds in London were sued for libel by the multinational corporation, the two sued back and the international vegan and vegetarian movement—including the Physicians Committee for Responsible Medicine in the U.S.—rallied to their support, turning the attack into an opportunity to make public the deceptions involved in McDonald's advertising and image making. The *Daily Telegraph* called the drawn-out trial "the best free entertainment in London." (McDonald's has become butcher to the world; more people get beef from McDonald's than from any other single source. Every day three new McDonalds open somewhere on the planet. See Appendix C: Organizations for the McLibel support committee.)

A fun, entertaining, moving, informative, and generally upbeat vegan video, "Truth or Dairy," produced by the Vegan Society of the U.K., features k.d. lang, Kate Pierson, Keith Strickland, Fred Schneider (B52s), Bryan Adams, River Phoenix, Philip Steir (Consolidated), Heather Small (M-People), Martin Shaw, Uri Geller, Casey Kasem, and a variety of women and men star athletes, along with music and an appearance by Moby. It's narrated by, and stars, U.K. Rastafarian poet Benjamin Zephaniah, who reminds us that:

> *Our power as consumers cannot be underestimated. We effectively dictate exactly what goods are produced. And as the demand for animal products starts to disappear, then the industries will have no choice but to start producing more ethically sound items or go bust. Really, when you think about it, becoming a vegan is the ultimate consumer boycott.*

14

Do It!

Whatever you can do or dream you can, begin it.
Boldness has genius, power, and magic in it.

GOETHE

It's been variously said that charity, peace, and revolution begin at home. But they certainly don't stop there. By changing our diets, and our consumption patterns in general, we begin the process of personal "empowerment"— the awareness and feeling that, individually and together, we can make a difference in the world. To switch to a plant-based diet is to take an effective stand against world hunger and species depletion, to help restore ecological balance, and to bring about social justice. That's a gift to ourselves, to others, and to future generations.

In addition, as citizens, we can get involved in the political process and incorporate food issues into it. We can encourage organic community gardens and farmers' markets in our communities. We can write letters to companies whose products we stop buying, telling them why. We can lobby for changes in the tax laws to encourage more responsible and ethical business practices. We can tell our representatives we want tax breaks for organic farmers, removal of current subsidies of animal agriculture and to-bacco, and the cutoff of aid to foreign governments that ruthlessly suppress every attempt of their citizens to gain control over the land. We can patronize organic producers, encourage them to go veganic, and ask current "green ma-nure" and "stockless rotations" farmers to start calling themselves veganic. We can lobby for a veganic subcate-gory of the new national organic standards. Gardeners can plant fruit and nut trees and hardy vegetables in public-access places, as the Fruition Project in Santa Cruz, California does. We can work to establish whole-food plant-based meals in various institutions, patterned after the Santa Cruz public schools; the student cafeterias in major universities like Berkeley, Cornell, and Santa Cruz; many schools and all prisons in Britain; and Seventh Day Adventist hospitals worldwide. Teachers can integrate plant-based nutrition programs into school curricula, while parents and students can work for healthy, plant-based alternatives in school lunch programs. One former multimillionaire rancher, Howard Lyman, had transformed his inherited traditional family farm into an agribusiness machine but saw the error of his ways during a personal health crisis; he now crisscrosses the country promoting veganism. The possibilities are limited only by our imagi-nations and our political will.

In a time of increasing homelessness, poverty, and cut-backs in government social assistance, most private chari-ties feeding the hungry and homeless seem not to take into account animal rights, ecology, or the health effects of ani-mal foods on humans. There are a few exceptions, though. In New York City, the Whole Foods Project feeds thousands of organic, vegan meals each year to hungry people. Food

Not Bombs, a network of independent groups in dozens of U.S. cities and now abroad, feeds vegetarian, often vegan and organic, food to the homeless in highly visible places while making the connection between high military spending, cutbacks in social support services, and increasing social problems. Volunteers working with Plenty help poor people around the world and here at home develop food self-sufficiency. In several cities Seventh Day Adventists operate vegetarian free meal programs and Hare Krishna groups operate mobile vegetarian kitchens. In San Francisco, a full third of the free meal programs— six out of eighteen—provide vegetarian-only food or vegetarian alternatives; two are vegan.

Bringing it all home, we can "think globally, eat locally," voting for the kind of world we want every time we shop, spend, or save.

We have a limited time in this life and each of us has a unique set of skills, talents, and characteristics to bring to the task of making a more livable place for all life. Even our most difficult or painful experiences are valuable, teaching us things that we wouldn't otherwise know, things that can help us be more powerful in the world if we incorporate and learn from the pain and rise above it. In the process of living more and more fully, we have the chance to learn to balance passion with equanimity. As one song by Deena Metzger about the danger of nuclear war puts it:

There is time only to work slowly
There is no time not to love[1]

Moving deliberately, however, is not the same as passivity or being timid. It was the German philosopher Goethe who observed that:

Until one is committed, there is hesitancy, the
*   chance to draw back, always ineffectiveness.*

Concerning all acts of initiative
  there is one elementary truth
  the ignorance of which kills countless ideas
  and endless plans:
That the moment one definitely commits oneself,
  then Providence moves, too.
All sorts of things occur to help one
  that would never otherwise have occurred.
A whole stream of events issues from the decision,
  raising in one's favor
  all manner of unforeseen incidents
  and meetings and material assistance, which no
  one could have dreamed would come their way.
  Whatever you can do or dream you can, begin it.
Boldness has genius, power, and magic in it.

It's much more comfortable for both new vegetarians and their friends to operate as if the switch was made solely because of health considerations, even if it wasn't. Giving up unhealthy foods, while requiring a great deal of admirable self-discipline, is not the moral statement (and perceived challenge) that refusing to kill is.

We are sometimes reluctant to admit to our "softer" feelings for others, especially when those "others" are of a different species. Men have a hard time with this because of social conditioning—"big boys don't cry"—and women, tired of being stereotyped and trivialized as "emotional," sometimes cut themselves off from profound feelings of sympathy for (and identification with) suffering animals. Many of the major social problems we face—from environmental destruction to the threat of nuclear war—are related to our downplaying or denial of the emotional, empathetic parts of ourselves. In this light, our openness to the suffering of others, human and nonhuman, is a joyous gift to a callused world, nurturing the best in us all.

A disturbing part of our cultural heritage actually denies animal suffering. The renowned philosopher René Descartes viewed animals as unfeeling "biological machines." In a classic case of delusion, early vivisectors, following Descartes' lead, would nail dogs to the wall and cut them up alive, dismissing their convulsions, whimpers, and screams as mere mechanical reactions, like a clock striking the hour. With traditions like this, it's no wonder that some people still believe that nonhuman animals don't feel pain—except for their own pets, of course!

To stay in the vegetarian closet is to deny a precious gift to a world sorely in need of it. Within each of us, an insecure clinging to the present exploitative order coexists with the yearning for a better way. A healthful, ecological, nonviolent diet is part of that better way. Clear, honest, nonpreachy answers to questions like "Why don't you eat meat?" or "Why don't you do dairy?" nurture change and can, with time, transform the people around you. Don't believe it? Give it a try.

15

Getting There

S ome people like the decisiveness of going "whole hog" with dietary change, going overnight from pork chops to plant foods. Others, instead of plunging in, would rather dabble their toes in the water first, making a more gradual change: giving up meat first, then eggs, then milk, allowing the body to transition to a more natural diet over a period of weeks, months, or longer. One advantage of the whole-hog approach is to avoid the pitfall that many new vegetarians fall into, namely, increasing the amount of cheese and other milk products that they use.

Some people do experience discomfort (usually a longing for old, familiar foods) when making the switch to any new eating pattern. When this happens in response to giving up meat or dairy products, many people think, "I'm not getting enough protein" and go back to the meat or dairy products. But the discomfort has nothing to do with protein, assuming that you eat concentrated sources of vegetable protein like beans and tofu. If the cause of the discomfort is physiological, it may be that you've suddenly decreased, say, your fat intake, and your body craves it. You can relieve the symptoms by substituting vegetable oils, but this is advisable only in a transition period, because high levels of either animal or vegetable fats are not healthful.

More likely, though, the cause is psychological, or a mix of mental and physical. Our attachment to certain tastes, smells, and textures of food is a strong one, and even relatively small changes from the familiar set of sensory inputs can cause temporary feelings of not being satisfied, of not feeling full. Some people are lucky and don't experience this, but, with our strongly animal-based American diet, quite a few of us do react this way when giving up meat or dairy products.

It's also possible your body is purging itself of impurities accumulated over years of improper eating. Whatever the cause, what do you do about it, other than throwing in the towel and going back to your old dietary ways?

Be patient, don't panic. Hang in there, with both humor and determination. Experiment with different foods and eating patterns. Avoid teasing yourself with the foods you want to give up. If you have generally supportive friends or family members, ask if they'll eat vegetarian or vegan with you when you eat together, just to support you in your transition. Join a vegetarian support group, or form your own formal or informal one (write the North American Vegetarian Society or the Vegetarian Resource Group for "how to" information; see Appendix C: Organizations); even one other person on the same path can provide valuable support. Read books, learn or relearn how to cook, subscribe to magazines like *Vegetarian Journal* and *Vegetarian Times* (see Appendix A: Further Information). If there are well-known singers or political leaders who follow the diet you aspire to and who you admire or find sexy, you might put up pictures of them for a while to remind yourself of the positive nature of what you're doing. Use transitional ("icon") foods, maybe even oily ones for a while; using vegetable oils to wean yourself from animal fats is a bit like using methadone to get off heroin—it can be a valuable transitional tool, but can itself be addictive. The ultimate goal, from a health viewpoint, is to get to a lowfat diet.

If you tend to view healthy eating as an unappetizing "bark and grass" affair, buy one of the many vegetarian or vegan cookbooks that cater to your desire for sinfully indulgent and filling meals; reviews in vegetarian publications will often let you know this, or you can call a local or national vegetarian organization and ask. If you develop a craving for sweets as a pleasure compensation for the familiar food you're giving up, try to indulge it as healthfully as possible, say, with sweet, ripe peaches or mangoes instead of sugary chocolates (concentrated sweeteners drain calcium from the body and weaken the immune system).

Give yourself lots of vegetarian or vegan foods that are both healthful and luscious; reinforcement with pleasure is powerful, and an important part of any transition. You may find that imagining the creature an animal food came from helps strengthen your resolve not to use that food anymore. If you feel intimidated about shopping in natural foods stores, relax. Just browse around, and don't feel that any question is too basic to ask. People who work there are used to "new" people coming in; most are more than willing to answer any questions.

And hang in there, knowing that you're strong and capable of making positive change in your life. Don't be hard on yourself if you backslide now and then; just renew your resolve to forge ahead. After all, "two steps forward, one step backward" is still good progress. Keep in mind the tremendous change you're making. In our modern world, heavy meat eating is still considered by many to be part of the good life, and the whole of human civilization has in large part been based on animal exploitation, sometimes out of felt necessity. The very fact that you've started on this vegetarian journey is a pretty amazing thing, when you think about it.

When we first stop eating a food we're used to, it often feels like we're giving up something precious, making a great sacrifice, but then we discover a whole wonderful world of alternatives that we weren't aware of before. Actually, there are only a few kinds of animals that most people eat, while an enormous variety of vegetables, grains, beans, nuts, seeds, and fruits are available for satisfying pleasure-hungry taste buds. As time passes, the animal products we liked so much before lose their appeal and, for most, come to be unappealing, to put it mildly.

Your transition may happen gradually or immediately, or it may come as a "click" when a lot of information you've been accumulating and insights you've been developing suddenly coalesce; it happens in vegetarian transition just as in any sort of consciousness raising. However your change comes, know that your process is a familiar one repeated countless times in many lives. Whatever your diet is now, an exciting and rewarding journey lies ahead!

On that journey, most of us get to face the many ways we use and misuse food. We use it to nurture our bodies, for the pleasure it brings, and for the social life that often happens around it. We also let it substitute for other forms of nonfood nurturance we're not getting enough of. But if, for example, we're not getting enough touch, it's healthier, and more pleasurable, to get a hug or a massage or to wrestle with a friend than to squish more food over our taste buds than our stomach can handle.

We also use eating as a way to avoid uncomfortable feelings, letting us ease the pain much like drowning our troubles in alcohol. We wind up overstuffed, often with unhealthy foods, which undermines our health and with it our capacity to experience pleasure.

A few guidelines that I've discovered or been taught (I'm still learning) in my own ongoing struggle with food habits are:

- Forgive yourself. Don't beat yourself up for your dietary sins; remember that the original biblical word translated as "sin" actually means "missing the mark," which is another way of saying, "aim better next time." This includes not beating yourself up for falling off the wagon once in a while.

- Don't let forgiveness become laxness or rationalizations; dissolve both complacency and guilt simply by being aware of them when they arise.

- Try viewing food more as a sensual source of nurturance than as a tasty but unhealthy reward for being good or an austerely "healthy" punishment for yesterday's dietary sins.

- Don't eat foods that you don't like; rather, find foods that are enjoyable *and* healthy, including very sensual ones.

- Don't constantly tease yourself with foods that are bad for you, for animals, for the planet. Whether you go slowly or whole hog, when you give up a particular food, do so completely, selecting other foods that will give you plenty of pleasure as well as adequate nutrition.

- Nonfood pleasures are important: time with (or away from) your child; a long, luxurious bath or hot tub; a massage; time with friends; extra time with a special friend. Often it's those things we really want, anyway, but substitute food instead.

- Love and accept yourself enough to be able to extend that love to other embodied beings.

Unless you're lucky enough to have a live-in vegetarian cook or wealthy enough to eat in restaurants all the time, switching to a vegetarian way of *eating* may seem easier than learning new ways to *prepare* your food. You may not realize it, but if you're like most people, you're already eating a lot of vegetarian and even vegan foods, and others that can easily be made so by eliminating the meat, egg, milk, and so on, with or without substituting something else. These days, many people are eating more vegetarian-*ish* anyway; for them, such a shift is not a big one.

But what if you're a big meat eater or don't cook? Or what if you want to expand your limited vegetarian cooking repertoire? A good way to learn is from a friend, or together with a friend. If you don't know anyone who's interested in exploring vegetarian cooking, you can take classes in preparing vegetarian cuisine. Many Seventh Day Adventist churches offer cooking classes; look in your yellow pages under "Churches." Bulletin boards at natural and health food stores and co-ops are excellent places to look for notices of vegetarian cooking classes. (A "health food" store carries supplements such as vitamins, packaged natural food products, usually a refrigerated section, and perhaps a limited selection of fresh produce and/or bulk bin items. A "natural food" store has this plus a more extensive selection of produce and bulk-bin foods. Both are usually in the yellow pages under "Health Food.") Personal classified ads in local papers can help you link up with other vegetarians.

There's an avalanche of vegetarian—and now vegan—cookbooks available in health and natural food stores and bookstores, or you can order them by mail (see Appendix B: Recipe Books and Cookbooks). If you have a computer and a modem, an abundance of recipes, advice, and support lies waiting at your fingertips. Vegetarian organizations are standing by, ready to help.

All this leaves you little excuse, once the urge to get back to the garden is on you.

Oh taste, taste and see
How good is the fruit that falls from the tree
Oh taste, taste and see
How good is the fruit of the garden

Taste the sun, stored in the skin
Flavor of fire and of passion
Taste the stars that dwell at the core
Seed of our joy and compassion

Taste the rain soaked through the flesh
It lingers so sweet on the tongue
Taste the earth, the body of life
Dark and rich and strong.[1]

16

Icons

It's not just the taste, smell, and texture of foods that's important; it's their image as well. Once you've become vegetarian, you may find that an occasional meat eater—or vegetarian—will make fun of you if you eat "fake meats" like tofu hot dogs or veggie burgers or, when you go vegan, for indulging in "fake ice cream" made from soy or rice bases. Some vegetarians, on the other hand, cling to a concept of "purity" or "naturalness" to set themselves apart; looking down on vegetarians who eat "fake" meats, milk, and ice cream is one way to do that.

Before we become vegetarian, we may want "vegetarian food" to *look* vegetarian, not like meat. If we can maintain a clear separation of meat and nonmeat foods, we can maintain the "specialness" of meat as a justification (albeit a thin one) for the ecological and health damage that the production of animal foods produces and the animal suffering it requires.

Most new vegetarians start out relying heavily on such products and over time use them less and less. These foods help greatly in easing the transition to vegetarianism and are a vital part of the vegetarian movement. But they're not just about personal transition; they're tools for transforming our culture as well, tools which greatly increase our chances of success.

Our culture, like all cultures, has dietary icons—foods that look a certain way. For most Americans, our dietary icons include hot dogs, hamburgers, steaks, baloney, milk and cereal, and ice cream. Images of these foods are recorded deeply in our psyches as we grow from infancy to adulthood, through repeated exposure in the home and in the media. They permeate our culture, and there's no need to reject a cultural icon or practice *if* we can find a way to transform it, removing its negative impacts.

A positive development that came out of the slaughter of World War II—or, rather, out of the food rationing that accompanied it—was the development of plant-based foods that resembled meats in texture. After the war, the companies that had developed these products found a market among vegetarians. The makers of these "fake meats" have sharpened their skills over the intervening decades, and in recent years such products have proliferated along with the rise in interest in vegetarianism.

At a good natural food store, you can now find multiple brands of vegetarian, usually vegan, hot dogs, ham and turkey slices, Salisbury steaks, and a slew of other "meats." Most veggie-burgers imitate their flesh counterpart only in form, not in taste, but a few are so authentically meat-like that some vegetarians find them "disgusting." The blossoming variety of "meaty" vegetarian foods is rivaling "the real thing" in variety of taste and texture, making the view of them as "meat substitutes" obsolete. In addition, there are prepared, packaged products made from tempeh, tofu, or wheat gluten that have no equivalent in the limited world of meat; we've developed beyond imitation and into initiation, as plant foods take the lead.

For your morning cereal, you can do your body far better with one of the variety of flavors of soy milk or rice milk, which you can use also in cooking just like cow's milk (actually, it's *calves'* milk when you think about it), but with far less fat. If you don't want to go to the store, you can make almond or cashew milk at home by throwing nuts (preferably soaked) and water into a blender, or a food processor with a metal blade. There are nondairy, plant-based "cheeses"—beware though—many are high fat, or contain casein or casseinates, milk products). Eggs can be replaced with packaged egg replacers, applesauce, mashed banana or tofu, or a little oil, depending on the recipe. One cookbook on the market, *The Uncheese Cookbook*, is devoted entirely to nondairy cheese cooking, with most of the recipes having no added oil. You can get nondairy yogurt and frozen yogurt, and the number of rice- and soy-based ice creams has multiplied in recent years, coming in various flavors in pints or quarts, push-ups, or on a stick, coated with chocolate or carob and, if you like, rolled in nuts.

In fact, there's nothing about most icon foods that makes them inherently animal based—burgers and ice cream can just as easily be made from soybeans and rice milk as from cow's meat and milk.

You also don't need to limit yourself to what you find in the store; use your imagination. For example, there were several brands of vegan cashew "cheese" spread/dip in the natural food store near my home, but they all had substantial quantities of added oil, on top of the cashews themselves being high in fat. So I wrote down the ingredients, went home, experimented, and came up with a specialty that wows most adults and some children.

Vegan Cashew Pimiento Cheese

Ingredients:

$1/2$ to 1 cup water

2 cups raw, unsalted cashew pieces

4-ounce jar of diced or sliced pimientos

3 tablespoons Red Star brand nutritional yeast flakes[1]

1 to 2 tablespoons lemon juice, or to taste

3 tablespoons sesame salt[2] (or $1/2$ teaspoon salt)

Put $1/2$ cup water and the rest of the ingredients in a food processor or blender. Pulverize at high speed for several minutes (depending on the efficiency of the machine). Add additional water only if and as needed to keep the mixture moving. When thoroughly pulverized, serve chilled or at room temperature as a spread, dip, or condiment.

And while we're on recipes, here's another widely shared "secret" for nondairy ice cream. Take very ripe bananas (with plenty of black spots on the skins), peel, freeze well, cut into thin slices or small pieces, put in a food processor with a metal blade, and pulverize until the bananas become a thick, creamy ice cream that will astound the most unweaned friends. "Pulsing" the machine at first may work best, and you may need to stop a few times to scrape the banana off the sides of the container and down into the blades. Other frozen fruits or juices can be put in with the banana to yield various colors and flavors, or used on their own for sorbet.

In short, the vegan revolution is upon us, and it's a lot easier to get on board today than it was just a few years ago. Once you make the change, don't let people who still eat meat or drink milk lay exclusive claim to our cultural/dietary icons. They belong to all of us. And the plant-based ones are better—for us, for the animals, and for the planet.

17

Vege-Babes

A person may be vegetarian or vegan, but still have qualms about raising their kids that way. "I have the right to decide for myself," they reason, "but I don't have the right to make that decision for my child. And maybe she *needs* milk."

Yes, she does—*mother's* milk, until she can switch to plant foods. Cow's milk is for calves. Babies and kids on a plant-based diet tend to be healthier and thinner than their meat-eating counterparts, but even dedicated vegetarians and vegans can have their commitment shaken by dire warnings of misguided friends or nutritionally uninformed doctors about what will happen if the baby doesn't get enough protein, or calcium, or whatever—legitimate concerns, but often misplaced. But let's back up a bit.

Babes in the womb do need calories and protein, meaning their moms have to eat a bit more than usual. Given our cultural patterns of overeating, that's generally not a problem unless the mother is undernourished or bulimic. A source of vitamin B-12 is crucial, and iron supplementation may be advisable during the second half of the pregnancy (B-12, and supplementation in general, will be dealt with later). See the New Four Food Groups chart in chapter 5, "Gimme Four," for plant sources of needed calcium. In general, vegetarian moms tend to have *healthier* babies than their meat-eating counterparts, since they usually have more vitamin A and fiber in their diet, and are less likely to have deficiencies of zinc, folic acid, and iron (the extra vitamin C in vegetarians' diets helps the absorption of iron). (See Appendix A: Further Information, for books on pregnancy, birthing, and child rearing.) Folic acid is more likely to be in abundance in a vegetarian diet; a deficiency is thought to cause birth defects.

One of the studies that have shown the advantages of a healthy vegan diet for pregnant moms and their babies followed 1,700 vegan pregnancies in a large vegan community in Tennessee called The Farm:

> *The study showed a record of safety that would de-light obstetricians. Only one in a hundred delivered by cesarean section. And in twenty years, there was only one case of preeclampsia, a syndrome of hypertension, fluid retention, urinary protein loss, and excessive weight gain that occurs in at least 2 percent of pregnancies in the United States overall. Other studies found similar results.*[1]

In addition, it's important to avoid alcohol, smoking, fats, refined sugars, and junk food generally, and to stay away from fish for a few *years* before *conceiving;* the high levels of toxins concentrated in the bodies of sea creatures can cause deformities and interfere with normal development.

Once the baby's out, mother's milk has nutrients that boost immunity. Cow's milk, on the other hand, can cause colic and allergies, and is indirectly implicated in insulin-dependent diabetes and sudden infant death syndrome. Cow's milk contains what's good for calves to grow on, plus high concentrations of agricultural poisons (pesticides and herbicides), which are bad for the babies of both humans and cows. If breast feeding is impossible, commercial soy formulas (*not* regular soy milk from the store) are a good substitute; hospital nurseries are accustomed to using them.

After three months, but not before, babies need an iron-rich diet. As a child grows, he needs protein, but not in the quantities that Americans consider high. And while kids also need some fats in the diet, the problem with American children generally is an *excessive* intake with resultant health problems. Vitamin B-12 is important; see chapter 21 "Common Concerns" in this book.

It's much easier these days to raise a child vegetarian or vegan, but it's still not always easy, thanks to social pressures accentuated by advertising for animal foods. It's not only that the commercials on children's TV programs push unhealthy foods, but the healthy looking on-screen hosts or characters mention high-fat foods, sweets, and meats like hot dogs and hamburgers far more often than healthier fruits or vegetables. (An exception is Mister Rogers, himself a vegetarian.)

To deny foods like hot dogs, burgers, or ice cream to children, who are subject to tremendous peer pressure, is to cut them off from their culture and their playmates. But these days, parents don't have to make the cruel choice anymore between providing a healthy, humane diet on the one hand and, on the other, foods that their children's playmates eat. The hot dog monster that emerges in most American kids can today be fed with any of a wide variety of soy- and wheat-gluten-based frozen, refrigerated, or canned hot dogs; there are burgers galore; and the ice

cream monster can be satiated with any of a variety of sinfully delicious plant-based ice creams.

When it comes to food, parents have no responsible
choice but to decide for their child. They must make the
best decision they can, based on the information they
have—*and on their values*. It's important to give children as
healthy a start as possible in the world, and also to support
and encourage their caring, nurturing instincts. A plant-
based diet scores highest on both counts.

Once your kid's in school, at least one meal a day will
be away from home. School lunches, while providing
regular meals to children, some of whom might not have a
meal at all otherwise, are still notoriously high in fat and
sodium, and generally unhealthful. An individual solution,
of course, is to prepare a lunch for your child to take. But
some parents have had remarkable success in getting
schools to provide vegetarian and vegan alternatives (see
the *Healthy School Lunch Action Guide*/EarthSave in
Appendix C: Organizations). It's more work in the short
run, but over the long run it saves you time and money, allows your child to be able to eat with their playmates, benefits all the children in the school, not just yours, and sets
an example for parents of children in other schools.

> *I may not be able to ban slaughterhouses and battery
> farms from the world, but I can ban them from my life.*
> A 17-YEAR-OLD GIRL

The up-and-coming generation is inheriting a planet
more ecologically ravaged than it was for previous generations. A large part of the reason for this is animal agriculture,
so it's not surprising that young people today are the most
vegetarian-oriented generation yet. Modern youth have one-
upped their parents' hippy generation by going not only
vegetarian but vegan in increasing numbers. 'Zines (home-
produced magazines) write about vegan food and animal

rights, while veganism is widespread among the smoke-free, alcohol-free, drug-free, straight-edge set. Vegetarian rock singers and groups sing about animal rights, and you can see previously leather-clad punkers sporting animal-free clothing and going vegan. Small, often funky, sometimes creative, vegan cookzines selling for a few dollars circulate through this thriving vegan youth subculture.

As a cultural phenomenon, veganism is today where vegetarianism was in the 60s. But unlike the vegetarians of their parents' generation, who usually had vague ideas about health and "naturalness" behind their vegetarianism, Generation V (for "vegan" or "vegetarian") is strongly motivated by very pointed concerns about animal rights, the spiritual implications of participating in massive abuse, and ecological destruction. As one teen was quoted in *Vegetarian Times* magazine, "I think it's really messed up when one species [humans] can cause so much damage."

The number of Americans who say they're vegetarian has increased from seven million in 1986 to over twelve million today, and teens are on the cutting edge of this cultural shift. Eighty percent of them consider environmentalism to be "in," and a full 25 percent feel that way about vegetarianism. Some young people make their commitments not only without support, but in the face of hostility in their families or circle of friends, or they may live in an area where there's little nutritional awareness. The problems vegeteens face from nonvegetarian family members led freelance writer Judy Krizmanic to write the book *A Teen's Guide to Going Vegetarian.* Animal rights organizations from PETA to the Antivivisection Society have started up youth groups, and the quarterly teen journal *How On Earth!*, published by the Vegetarian Action Network, is read by thousands around the country, with a subscription list growing by the month. Members of YES!, a group of young people affiliated with EarthSave, go on tours around the country speaking to schools about environmental issues, including the various benefits of vegetarian and vegan diets; they also organize camps and empowerment workshops. The Healthy School Lunch Project of EarthSave has produced the *Healthy School Lunch Action Guide* to help parents, kids, and other concerned people work to institute vegan alternative meal lines in school cafeterias.

High schoolers are also often confronted with dissection in biology class, as are college students in life sciences. The last decade has seen a swell of student conscientious objectors, with the result that four states have passed laws requiring schools to offer alternatives to students who object to dissection. Elementary, high school, and college level students who don't want to dissect can get information and support by calling a national toll-free number (see Dissection Hotline in Appendix C: Organizations).

```
Message-ID: <9401261431.AA05632@wol.com>
To: jjones@vvt.com
Subject: on the way!

hi julie,

i finally told my folks i was going vegan.
they weren't very happy about it, but
after i showed them the printed stuff you
sent, mom sorta came around. dad's still
not convinced, and they're trying to get
me to "at least" do eggs and milk, but it
looks like I'm going to have an easier
time of it than you did.

thanks for the info and the inspiration. later.

in vegan love and peace,

frankie-boy
```

The University of California at Berkeley not long ago instituted a full vegan alternative meal line in all six of its dormitory cafeterias, as a result of student pressure and diplomacy. (See Appendix G: Getting Vegan Food in Institutions for their organizing paper.) Vegetarian and vegan meal *items* had been offered for years, but now there's full meal service every day—for breakfast, lunch, and dinner. The campus restaurants also offer vegan options.

Berkeley was not the first to do this. They were preceded by Cornell University, the University of California at Santa Cruz, the University of Washington, and a number of private schools.

While this may seem at first like a radical change, if you consider all the health benefits of a plant-based diet, and all the health, ethical, and ecological problems associated with the use of animal products, it's surprising that our educational institutions have taken as long as they have to begin to see the light. Said one student in a radio interview, "If they had veganism offered on the stock market, I'd put all of my money into it, because its going nowhere but up."

> *I can tell you it's easier today. When I became vegetarian in my twenties, I was considered kinky. Not so today.*
> A FEMALE ELDER

The advantages of a vegetarian diet are legion. In fact, the only problem that has been raised is that it's *such* a healthy way of eating that vegetarians, and especially vegans, because of living much longer, may be more likely to live to be old enough to need rest home or nursing home care in their final years. (A nursing home has round-the-clock medical staff; a rest home does not.) In our youth-oriented, shun-the-elders, die-in-the-hospital-or-nursing-home culture, growing old can be a trying experience for many. This is especially so for vegetarians, and most especially for vegans.

Rest homes can hire anybody to do the cooking, even the janitor. The result can be great home-cooked food, or a nutritional and gustatory disaster. In any case, unless they're owned by a vegetarian person or organization, rest homes are not likely to be vegetarian friendly, and even less likely vegan friendly, unless such arrangements are made with a sympathetic kitchen staff. (For example, Sunset Hall, a rest home in Los Angeles for retired radicals and free-thinkers of various sorts, is not vegetarian, but will keep vegetarian or vegan food for any resident that requests it. See Appendix G: Getting Vegan Food in Institutions.)

Nursing homes, on the other hand, are required by federal law to have a dietitian, and to satisfy the dietary preferences of all residents, whether they're "mere" taste preferences or represent a religious, moral, or philosophical commitment. Few people are aware of this legal right. Knowledge is power.

If a nursing home fails to give a resident food in accordance with their cultural needs and personal choice—or in any other way violates their rights—the federally mandated Long-Term Care Ombudsman may be able to help. Each state must have at least one, whose sole duty is to defend the rights of the elderly in nursing and retirement homes and home-care Meals On Wheels recipients. Most states have more than one ombudsman, usually located in Area Agencies on Aging, legal aid programs, or even consumer organizations. California has 35 locations, each with at least one ombudsman assisted by trained volunteers who make unannounced visits to homes. If you can't find the ombudsman for your area, contact the program's national office (see Appendix G: Getting Vegan Food in Institutions).

The big nursing home chains have publicly stated policies of catering to both vegetarians and vegans, while homes operated by the Seventh Day Adventist church (which advocates but doesn't require vegetarianism for its members), or by lay Adventists, are knowledgeable about vegetarian nutrition. Many other nursing homes are following suit, or will do so when faced with an informed and insistent resident—or their friends outside.

A vegan community in rural Tennessee is developing Rocinante, a 100-acre combination retirement and nursing home and midwife facility. The idea is that this will help avoid the segregation of elders into age ghettos and integrate them with children and families, with all the benefits of human touch and loving hearts.

"The Farm is spiritual," says the project's initiator, "but not religious. We don't follow any particular doctrine. We just believe in the obvious spirit that exists between all people."

Although not a substitute for flesh-and-blood company, emailing and teleconferencing can help counter the isolation of seniors or anyone living segregated off or alone, and it's exciting to chat almost instantaneously with people all over the world. Online discussion groups include vegetarianism, veganism, lowfat diets, and veggie menus for institutions. And what better way for a lone vegetarian in an uncooperative nursing home to develop and share strategies with distant others in similar circumstances? The number of nursing home residents on the Internet is increasing as computer literacy spreads, as online access becomes more user friendly, and as both veggie boomers and cyber boomers age and begin to enter eldercare institutions.

In Europe, there are *cohousing* communities especially for the elderly. So far there are none in the United States, but some of the design characteristics of cohousing, which encourage both independence and social interaction, are beginning to be imitated by some institutions for the elderly. Meanwhile, multigenerational cohousing projects continue to be developed here (see Appendix C: Organizations), and at least one has made design provisions for elderly members. By keeping people socially connected, these housing alternatives are conducive to keeping people healthy. Social isolation, which plagues many but especially the elderly, is directly correlated with mental, social, and physical problems. A move into cohousing—along with good nutrition and plenty of aerobic and weight-bearing exercise—might help you stay healthier as you grow older. Many cohousing communities accommodate vegetarians, and recently there have been initiatives to establish vegetarian or vegan common meals in such communities.

Vegetarian taxpayers support senior meals programs, but are effectively excluded from them by lack of vegetarian or vegan entrees on the menus. But even this bastion of animal food diets is beginning to be affected by the revolution in eating habits, as the new crop of elders is requesting more healthy foods, and an old regulation limiting use of "meat alternatives" to once a week has been tossed out. This unlocks the door, but it's up to veggie-boomers and their friends to open it, applying friendly but unmistakable pressure to local programs and their superiors up the bureaucratic chain of command, addressing it as a health and health-care issue, a personal choice issue, and an economic issue—the wise use of limited funds to feed as many people as healthily as possible. Strategies used by young people to get vegan meals in universities can be adapted to get the same result with Meals On Wheels. In some places, groups feeding poor people of all ages are providing vegetarian or vegan food. (See Appendix G: Getting Vegan Food in Institutions, for a list of resources for vegetarian elders.)

18

Standing Your Ground

*All truth passes through three stages. First, it is
ridiculed. Second, it is violently opposed. Third, it is
accepted as being self-evident.*

SCHOPENHAUER

Lacto- and/or ovo-vegetarianism is still weird to some
people, but in many social circles and parts of the country
it has largely been accepted into the mainstream as a
valid, even admirable, personal choice. If you're vegan,
you're much more likely to meet incredulity from others,
although that, too, is changing. Until plant-based diets become more fully accepted, how do you deal with the flak
you get about your dietary choices?

There are several things that make for good, effective
communication with people who ridicule you or challenge
your choice of diet. These principles seem to apply to other
areas of life as well.

First, if possible, establish a relationship with the person before the challenge is made. Or find commonalities,

even such things as being from the same state. Connect with them around any- and everything that will help them to see you (and you them) as a person, not an enemy or an "other."

Second, talk "with" them, not "to" them, in their language. If they're timid and shy, speak softly and gently. If they're intellectual, present them with facts and academic arguments. If they're sharp-tongued and disdain other modes of relating, try lashing into them with your wit.

Third, validate anything you can about them, their beliefs, their actions, and so on. What have they said or what do you know they believe that relates to the subject at hand? Even if you have to stretch it, find *something* good to say about them, but by all means don't be fake about it.

Fourth, continue to be the kind of person they like to be around, not because you're slavishly dependent on their approval (a surefire way to torpedo communication), but because it will feel better to you—it will be pleasure-positive.

Fifth, know your subject and be able to cite a wide variety of sources that a range of people will accept as impressive. Conservative sources work best—if the USDA or the Meat Board says a vegetarian diet is okay, that's more impressive than if a vegetarian society says it.

Sixth, use lateral thinking, finding parallels between your issue and other issues you know are important to them. This can give them insight in an area they've not explored or taken seriously before.

Seventh, listen to them, and make it obvious that you're doing so. Don't be condescending or patronizing. If they don't feel preached at, they're more likely to listen to you. But you have to be *really* willing to listen, including being ready to admit to any confusion, uncertainty, or contradictions in your own position.

A good example of how ridicule is used to put down people who choose liberational paths—and how a good communication strategy can be effective in responding—appeared in "Savage Love," a nationally syndicated sex advice column written by Dan Savage and appearing in Seattle's *The Stranger*. Renowned for his sharp tongue and graphic language, Dan used one of his columns to lash into vegans:

"Vegans are tiresome," he wrote. "They're annoying, to say nothing of impossible to cook for. Every vegan I've ever known has been a slo-mo anorexic: 'Oh, no; can't eat that.' 'No, thank you; that has cheese in it.' 'Eek! Yogurt!' 'Is there butter in this? Oh, well: I'll just sit here in the corner and eat this little pile of birdseed.'"

In a subsequent issue of the paper, he noted that he'd been deluged with mail from angry vegans, all of which he dismissed as "tear-smudged, five-page letters about how betrayed and violated you felt." Except one, which came from his own proofreader, Sara DeBell, who challenged him on his own terms, in his own language, generating his respect as "the least pathetic and most informed response to my vegan-baiting." He printed her letter.

"I love you for your big mouth, your loose tongue and your rapier wit—but, honey, you don't know about vegans. One in three Americans is obese. Dan, they ain't vegans (and vegans don't get acne on their butts, either). Despite appearances, we vegans are not 'slo-mo anorexics'—we don't need to be. We can eat all that we want—full, hot luscious meals and mouth-watering desserts—and we don't gain weight. That's because we *eat right*. Meat and dairy eaters are slo-mo heart attacks. One in two Americans dies of heart disease, which is only one direct result of our animal-based diet. Two others are cancer and diabetes. The reasons vegans are so difficult to dine with is that most restaurants serve noxious crap. Your vegan friends might settle for a green salad (or 'bird seed') because that's the only item on the menu not laden with saturated fat, overburdened with protein, and short on the fiber that keeps our butts so clean. It's not easy for vegans to eat out.

"This country's tastes and values have been set by a money-hungry USDA—the inventors of the four food groups we grew up with, which still dominate our thinking—assigned (and paid with taxpayer dollars) to promote meat and dairy foods. The USDA knows—and they knew in 1956, when those heinous, morbid four food groups made their debut—that the products they promote sicken us. This is not an impartial, consumer-friendly organization, Dan. You're brainwashed, my friend, and by the government, which subsidizes and promotes cattle ranchers and dairy farmers just as it promotes and protects tobacco farmers. The American Heart Association, the American Diabetes Association, and the American Cancer Society don't take a stand because they're big and unwieldy, hence ruled by politics, and don't want to lose their funding. If you only knew the well-concealed facts (the American diet not only wreaks havoc on our bodies, it is also decimating the global environment), you'd be just as adamant about this scourge as you are about cigarette smoking. Further reading: Neal Barnard, M.D.; John McDougall, M.D.; Dean Ornish, M.D.; and the Pulitzer-nominated (albeit New Age prissy) John Robbins.

"Love,

"Your Proofreader."

Sara the proofreader got through where others didn't. Dan's printed response to her letter, while still sarcastic, was decidedly toned down this time around, and he even let drop that his lover was vegan. How did Sara get through?

• The personal relationship between the two provided a framework within which the conflict could take place.

• She used his language, the sort of graphic imagery and sharp tongue that he would use; this approach got far more of his attention and respect than the "tear-smudged" letters of others.

• She validated the things she liked about him at the beginning; she stated clearly where she felt he was "off."

• She used lateral thinking, making parallels between her issue and an issue she knew to be important to him (smoking). She gave him sources of information he would respect.

• And she remained, throughout her attack on his position, a person who in his eyes was a fun person to be around—and spar with.

If your dietary decision represents deep-seated values, you may find it harder to deal with people *downplaying* your motives than with outright ridicule. "You eat plants; I eat animals. Everything's okay." When faced with people who diffuse your commitment by packaging it as a dietary "preference" or "choice," you don't have to do anything, just know that your example speaks volumes. Or, without sounding (or being) smug about it, you can remind them that for you it's not just a *preference,* but a *commitment,* like anyone's commitment to something important to them, be it honesty and good communication, financial solvency, supporting a family, social justice, animal rights, good health, or a cleaner environment. Also notice any areas where their lives reflect more awareness, consciousness, or maturity than does yours. We all tend to develop unevenly: some of us in one area, others in another. A vegan may commute by car hours a day, polluting the common air, while a meat eater may be very dedicated in biking or taking the bus or train. A dedicated social change activist may be alienating people with her approach, while her friend may be skilled in interpersonal communication but lack an understanding of broader issues. We can learn from each other. The more open I am to learning from you in your specialty areas, the more open you'll be to learning from me. We need all the skills and talents that each of us has.

Almost all of us vegans and vegetarians can easily remember a time when we weren't. We weren't stupid or evil. We were just ignorant, or bound by habit, or both—and both are shored up by the huge advertising budgets available to the animal foods industries.

As much as we may sometimes feel frustration or despair with our own kind, as human beings we have the potential to give to each other in ways not possible with other life forms.

19

CyberVeg:
Vegetarianism on the Infobahn

The well-publicized information superhighway is not only for game players and Internet surfers with no other life; it can be a powerful tool for vegetarians to network with each other and to spread the word.

The groundwork for the Internet was laid by the U.S. military–industrial complex. They figured that a decentralized computer communications network would be more likely to survive a nuclear war. What they apparently didn't foresee was how, as it grew beyond the military, government agencies, and research institutes it originally served, it would also allow grassroots individuals and organizations to "plug in" to the system with minimal oversight from centralized, for-profit corporations. The result is what's been called a global electronic democracy. That's a considerable overstatement; there's no voting, there are current and looming battles over such issues as control of access, sexual harassment, and sexual and political censorship, and not everyone can afford the hardware and a monthly bill for Internet access. Still, cyberspace *is* a new frontier in communications.

Vegetarians have been right in the thick of it all, and as a result there are a number of vegetarian and vegan pit stops on the infobahn. New, increasingly powerful, graphic, user-friendly click-and-go software is rapidly making full Internet access available to novice users who would be intimidated by having to type in arcane and convoluted commands. And with email, you can zap messages to like-minded people all over the world, almost instantaneously.

Which is not to say that computers, modems, and the Internet are this age's electronic version of the Father, the Son, and the Holy Ghost, though to some they seem to be. Electronic networking is a valuable tool and especially helpful to people who are shut in, isolated off from like-minded others, or involved in long-distance networking. I remember the excitement of a politically active friend who, during the crumbling of the Soviet Union, got blow-by-blow dispatches from Russian protesters who would end messages saying they had to log off to go clog the streets with their bodies because Soviet tanks had just been seen advancing on the Russian White House. But for people for whom computers are not a critical organizing tool, it can have the opposite effect: to the extent that they isolate us off from real relationships and life experiences, they represent precious time, life energy, irretrievably wasted. Online "relationships" are one-dimensional, and an easy escape from dealing with real, flesh-and-blood human beings. Many people have found computers to be addictive, so enter this area with all the awareness you can muster. If you wind up getting hooked anyway to the detriment of your real life, just pull the plug and start plugging back into the real world.

But let's assume that you're able to control the technology instead of letting it control you. If you're a member of one of the commercial providers such as America Online (AOL), you can participate in their forums on cooking (vegetarian subsection), philosophy, ecology, or animal rights. AOL also has a neat feature in member profiles, which any subscriber may choose to fill out. Any other member can search all these profiles for key words such as "vegetarian" or "vegan," read the complete profiles on all people with the key word in their profile, and initiate correspondence on the topic of mutual interest.

CompuServe's member magazine ran an article bordered by colorful fruit and vegetables with the headline "Vegan Revolution: Where You'll Find a Meatless Burrito Online." It described how the vegetarian section of the Cooks Online Forum became so crowded that a new, separate forum was created for it: the Vegetarian Forum. Just by word of mouth, before the official announcement, it had 200 members.

Many providers such as AOL, CompuServe, and Prodigy are implementing full Internet access, while others provide full access for a fixed monthly fee. If you're a student or teacher at a university or research institution, you may be able to get a free account. Some companies provide email accounts to employees who can use email in their line of work.

Electronic rendezvous in cyberspace can be especially valuable to vegetarians or vegans who feel isolated in their sentiments or their dietary choices. One such person, Bobbi Pasternak, lived without knowing another vegetarian at home, at work, or anywhere, until she discovered electronic networking. She's now the online resource person for the Vegetarian Resource Group, providing information and moral support to others.

See Appendix H: Vegetarian Online Resources for an extensive list of vegetarian resources on the Internet.

20

Money Talks

> *Cruelty is acknowledged only when profitability ceases.*
>
> RUTH HARRISON, *Animal Machines*

The love of it may be the "root of all evil," but money can be very helpful in paying the rent, so it's nice to know that a vegetarian—and especially vegan—way of eating saves bucks. Of course, it's possible to spend a lot more on gourmet vegetarian food than on the cheapest meats. What often happens when people become vegetarian and later vegan is that they start to become more health conscious; for example, they buy more natural, perhaps organically grown foods. The food bill can wind up being not so different than when they ate steak and pork chops. And if they start indulging in a lot of luxury foods, it might even be more. So their friends say, "Hmm . . . looks like this vegetarian idea can get expensive, I'd better stick to my meat and potatoes."

But if you want to save money, plant-based foods are the way to go. Supermarket veggies are cheaper than supermarket meats, organically grown plant foods are cheaper than organically grown animal foods, and a gourmet vegan or vegetarian meal will be cheaper than a similar one using gourmet meats. In every category of naturalness or how much you're splurging, plant foods come out the clear winner, leaving you not only with better health, a cleaner planet, and a clearer conscience, but also with money left over to spend on other things. For those of us not born to unlimited wealth, that's an important consideration.

The only exception to this rule is replacing meat, whose huge subsidies make it artificially cheap, with packaged "substitute" meats. Animal foods would be a lot more expensive than they are if they weren't heavily subsidized by the government, by our tax money. Perhaps the biggest such subsidy is through expensive federal projects to bring water to dry areas. Since most of the grains and soybeans grown with this subsidized water are fed to cows, pigs, and chickens in huge quantities, the water subsidy winds up being a subsidy of the meat, milk, and egg industry. For example, without this water subsidy—if farmers had to pay the full cost the irrigation projects to bring the water to grow the crops to feed the animals—hamburger would cost an estimated $35/pound and steak well over twice that. Or, more accurately, it *does* cost that much, but we pay part of the hidden cost at tax time, and pass the rest of the bill on to the environment and to future generations. The more vegan your diet is, the more you're off the welfare role of government subsidies.

A lot of creating a better world is determined by what we put into our mouths: animal or plant foods chemically, organically, or veganically produced by people trying to make an honest living versus those trying to make a quick buck. But we can also create a better world through more than just monitoring what we eat. We transport ourselves (bike vs. bus/train vs. car), pay taxes to implement government policies good and bad, save for children's education, or invest for retirement, personally or through pension plans at work. In general, banks and other money funds (including retirement systems) invest where the return is highest, with no thought to whether the project they're funding is healthy, ecological, humane, or conducive to strong and vibrant communities. The bottom line is profitability, and the highest profits, at least in the short run, may come from economic activities that do harm to animals, the ecosystem, individuals, or communities.

In recent years, some investors have begun thinking of themselves not just as "stockholders" but as "stakeholders," a term which acknowledges the personal stake all of us have in the welfare of each other and in the health of communities and the planet. Part of this change is the "socially responsible investment" (SRI) money funds that have sprung up like mushrooms after a rain. They try—or purport to try—to invest in things their investors believe in and to avoid investing in things like nuclear power, weapons production, environmentally destructive projects, companies with bad employee relations and those that discriminate on the basis of gender, race, or sexual preference.

One such social fund is Working Assets (also called Citizens Trust), founded by a vegetarian. Its current president, Sophia Collier, has been an ethical vegetarian for twenty-eight years, since she was eleven. She says Working Assets screens out companies such as McDonalds, Wendy's, Tyson Foods, and Luby's Steakhouse on grounds of animal welfare and that their products are not "good and useful."

"As I've grown older," says Collier, expressing a feeling common to many long-time, committed vegetarians, "I have been both encouraged by the growing awareness of the benefits of vegetarianism as well as disappointed that so few people make the commitment to become and stay vegetarian."

Social investing involves both positive and negative "screens." A *negative* screen disqualifies companies that are doing something you *don't* want to support. A *positive* screen seeks out companies that are doing things that you *do* want to support. A few of the SRI funds have *partial* negative screens for animal testing (painful, mutilating, or fatal experiments on live animals), but not for other forms of animal abuse. In other words, they (supposedly) won't invest in a company that tests on animals, but they might invest in one that uses or produces animal products, even as its main product or resource.

I don't know of any U.S. fund that has *comprehensive* screens—positive or negative—for animal rights, seeking out companies that take a leadership role in eliminating animal abuse or systematically eliminating all with any substantial involvement in animal exploitation. Many don't have any at all. Green Century, for example, says: "We don't have any kind of animal rights screen, just the environment."

In making investment decisions, most multi-issue social funds look at the overall picture and the general direction a company is headed; if the company scores well on, say, six of eight criteria, it will usually pass. When several issues are competing, animal issues tend to slide to the back burner, so that the animal screen gets enforced less than other screens. For example, when a potential investee has, say, good labor relations and is doing something positive for the environment, the tendency is to look the other way if it also does a "little" testing on animals. One social fund invested in a pharmaceutical company that does a *lot* of animal testing because it was otherwise socially responsible.

There are some points of light, however. New Alternatives decided against investing in a fish farming operation even though the project met its alternative energy criteria. When an animal-issue investor pointed out that one of their investees was involved in activities that hurt animals, they sold off that holding. Working Assets has a negative animal screen that goes beyond testing to exclude at least companies whose *primary* product is meat or those that treat animals cruelly in certain limited ways. It also claims to be the only fund to require companies to pass *all* its screens in order to qualify for investment.

But even Working Assets invests in supermarkets that sell meat, and one of its investees is Ben & Jerry's, the ice cream company that has a good reputation for employee relations and donates a good portion of before-tax profits to rain forest preservation efforts. Ben & Jerry's main resource is milk and they use tons of eggs each week. None of the ingredients is organic. The milk is from small farms, not factory farms, but "modern" dairy practices prevail, including the emotionally painful separation of cows from their calves shortly after birth, with the male calves going to veal production, while the mothers are presumably killed when their milk production goes down, rather than being allowed to die of old age.

> *I'm a mother. I have a pretty good idea of the kind of emotions that it would put me through to have somebody take my baby away from me. . . .There's no way anyone who has humanity or any compassion can take a calf away from its mother and think that that's all right.*
>
> CHRISSIE HYNDE, OF THE PRETENDERS[1]

The eggs that Ben & Jerry's uses are from chickens a lot less lucky than the cows; they're from out-and-out factory farms simply because that's the only source available for the quantities they use.

"Social investing is an incremental process," says the president of Working Assets, "and I am glad that we can find enough attractive companies to invest in so that we can eliminate businesses which are primarily merchants of meat. Some day we may be able to go further."

That time may be upon us. In the vacuum created by the lack of commitment to broad-spectrum animal rights by the large social funds, a small number of stockbrokers has been catering for a number of years to clients with concerns about animal exploitation. In the summer of 1995, Rocky Mountain Humane Investing was founded by a registered investment advisor applying a single-issue screen with varying degrees of strictness, from "humane society" standards (leather production okay, animal testing not) to ethical vegan. The strictness of the screen is tailored to the clients' needs and values; other screens (environmental, labor relations, etc.) can be applied on request. He and others feel frustrated by the way animal screens are so narrowly constructed and so half-heartedly implemented by SRIs. I experienced this myself when, shortly after being assured that Working Assets didn't invest in companies whose primary product was meat, I received their portfolio performance bulletin listing one of their investees as Lone Star Steak House and Saloon. When I contacted them about this, the president said she had also been horrified to see that stock appear in one of their portfolios; it had been bought by mistake, she said, and sold as soon as it was discovered. A question, though, remains: If this stock could slip in and then be discovered and eliminated, what about stocks of other companies that exploit animals in a major way that might slip in but not have such an obvious giveaway name? Might they remain in the portfolio, unnoticed? Welcome to the world of "socially responsible" investing.

It wasn't many years ago that there was no such thing as socially responsible investing. Only when the consciousness of enough people changed to give importance to things such as workers being treated right and the environment not being despoiled could the current crop of social investors take root and flower.

A similar increase of consciousness has been happening for a number of years about human abuse of animals and the impacts of animal-based diets on people, animals, and the planet. The large social investment funds haven't yet "got it," but the time seems to be ripening for one of them to get the jump on its competition by creating an *Ahimsa* portfolio for truly cruelty-free investment (not just avoiding animal testing). *Ahimsa* is Sanskrit for *nonviolence* or *harmlessness*. See chapter 9, "War and Peace."

SRIs are quick to claim that their positive and negative screens do not result in lower yields for their investors, pointing out that a fund's performance depends far more on the competence of the manager and her knowledge of the field than on any screens it might apply. So applying a comprehensive animal screen should be very possible—*if* there's a genuine interest in it. Because of the pervasiveness of animal products (used in plywood, rubber, and steel, for example), a line would have to be drawn somewhere; it could easily be drawn somewhere a lot more favorable to animals than what is currently the case. It should definitely exclude businesses in which animal products are more than an incidental part of their product or resources.

> The unnatural conditions of animal slavery are a short-ened life span, forced breeding, disruption of hormonal balance (as when a steer is injected with steroids to make muscle meat plumper), and separation of mother animals from their young. These should outrage the consciousness of any sensitive feminist.[2]

With all their shortcomings, the very existence of SRIs is causing people to think more about how their money is being used. In other words, a space has been created in which they are not only following changing social values, but are also taking leadership in the margins, expanding the frontiers from *social* responsibility to the broader realm of *ethical* and *cruelty-free* investing (although "cruelty-free" often gets misused to mean only no animal testing).

The multi-issue SRIs are plagued by several problems beyond the ones discussed above.

- Stakeholders, if they're thinking people, don't always fall neatly into progressive/conservative camps when it comes to attitudes toward the various social and ethical issues a fund attempts to address.
- There's a lack of clarity in distinguishing between such terms (and concepts) as socially responsible, ethical, and humane.
- The few funds that have any screens for animal rights or welfare define them too narrowly, for example applying them only for testing of personal care products, leaving open animal testing of products not for personal care or cruel experiments in the name of science, not to mention the many other forms of animal abuse.
- While it's easy to learn if a company does animal testing, it requires a certain amount of research— work—to root out other animal-exploiting activities, work that SRIs would rather not do.
- In avoiding animal testing, an SRI may use the "official USDA" definition of animal, which excludes a number of creatures like mice, guinea pigs, and poultry.
- "Animal rights," "animal welfare," or "cruel treatment" are defined far too narrowly. A fund may say (and perhaps believe) they are screening out "inhumane treatment of animals" when in actuality they're screening out only certain, limited, usually *noninstitutionalized* forms of abuse. The institutionalized forms, by definition, are those we have come to accept as normal, no longer shocking—and they are the forms causing the most suffering. For example, a fund's investors might be proud that they refused to

invest in a business that had deliberately and cruelly killed off a few hundred pesky animals around its facilities (especially if the business had gotten a lot of bad press about it), but still invest in supermarkets that sell the meat, eggs, and milk of tens of thousands of factory-farmed animals. (Part of the reason that such attitudes are widespread is because the large humane and antivivisection organizations have historically shied away from challenging the raising and killing of animals for food.)

- There is a confusion between "social" investing, which by definition is restricted to social (i.e., human) concerns, and "ethical" investing. Even environmental concerns are usually expressed in human-centered terms, as we worry about the quality of "our" environment but not about the other life-forms that inhabit it and consider it theirs, too. There are abundant *human-centered* reasons for not supporting animal agriculture, like health and a good environment, but animal agriculture's immediate, intentional, and primary victims—like the caged chickens laying eggs for Ben & Jerry's, or the calves separated from their mothers so humans can get the milk—are animals whose needs and rights can be systematically violated with impunity because they can't vote, speak human languages, boycott the process, or fight back successfully. The term "ethical investing" is much broader, more inclusive, and not necessarily limited to our own kind.

- There is no industry-wide, independent oversight and evaluation of the screens used by SRIs—the criteria they're based on and how strictly or consistently they're implemented—similar to the way that *Consumer Reports* evaluates products and manufacturers' claims, and in the way that organic farmers and consumer groups have hammered out industry-wide organic standards, gotten them implemented into law, and set up an overseeing group so that the public can know what a claim of "organic" means.

The following are SRI funds. As of press time, with the exception of Rocky Mountain Humane Investing (not a mutual fund like most of the rest on the list, but an independent money manager that doesn't comingle investors' funds), none had a comprehensive animal screen on any portfolio, but you can call and ask if they have plans to establish one. The more people who call—or, better yet, write—the sooner a company will create such a portfolio. If you find one you like, don't settle for general assurances or a list of example investments; get written statements setting forth in detail what they do and don't invest in, the specific criteria for a screen, and whether the screen is absolute (the investee must in all cases meet the criteria) or just weighted (considered or given weight in making the decision to invest or not).

Some of these funds are large, with a variety of portfolios, IRAs, tax deferred annuities, and so on. You might be able to get your employer to shift pension funds into a social fund or to offer you and other employees retirement options through an SRI fund. Other funds are small, with only simple, straightforward investing, like New Alternatives, perhaps the "greenest" fund, investing only in alternative energy.

If you invest in an SRI fund, your money will *not* be insured by the government, as it would be in a bank or savings and loan. Please note that a listing here does not in any way constitute an endorsement of a fund's fiscal soundness; before investing, consult your financial advisor. It also does not constitute an endorsement of their screens or their integrity. The listing is alphabetical.

Socially Responsible Investment Funds

Ariel	800-292-7435
Calvert	800-368-2748
Domini	800-762-6814
Dreyfus	800-782-6620
Green Century	800-934-7336
Laidlaw Covenant	800-275-2683
MMA Praxis	800-977-2947
Neuberger & Berman	800-877-9700
New Alternatives	800-423-8383
Parnassus	800-999-3505
Pax World	800-767-1729
Pro-Conscience	800-424-2295
Progressive Environmental Fund	800-367-7814
Rightime	800-242-1421
Rocky Mountain Humane Investing	800-678-3739
TIAA/CREF	800-842-2007
US Affinity	800-800-3030
Working Assets/Citizens Trust	800-223-7010[4]

Co-op America's *National Green Pages* (see Appendix A: Further Information) has listings under "Financial/ Investment Services" for other (including smaller and regional) social investment funds and individual investment brokers. The national organization of social investment companies in the U.S. is the Social Investment Forum (617-451-3369); in Canada, it's the Social Investment Organization (416-360-6047).

While the United States apparently has more money *socially* invested than any other country, the British lead in the comprehensiveness and range of criteria applied in *ethical* investing. This is especially true in the area of animal rights, on which the best of our SRIs are downright pathetic in comparison to some of their counterparts on the other side of the Atlantic. The Ethical Investors Group (EIG), a member of the U.K. Social Investment Forum, offers independent financial advice exclusively on ethical, including vegan-standard, investments.

The EIG encourages their affiliated investment companies to adopt—*and follow*—not only vegetarian and anti-testing, but vegan criteria. Many do. The EIG brochure "Cruelty-Free Money" states that the group seeks to avoid not only products tested on animals, but also strives to avoid any production, processing, or sale of dairy or meat products. Additionally, the EIG attempts to avoid companies that pollute, deal in weapons, support repressive regimes, or promote alcohol or tobacco.

Many of the EIG's clients are found outside the U.K. According to Coates, however, U.S. law forbids any U.S. citizen to receive even *advice* from any organization not registered as a U.S. investment company. Members of congress will change this law if and when they start getting letters and calls and email messages demanding a free flow of investment information. The EIG can be contacted for an update on the status of the law; they might also be encouraged to do whatever is necessary to register as a U.S. investment company.

Ethical Investors Group
Milestone, Greet Road
Greet, Cheltenham GL54 5BG
United Kingdom
Tel/Fax: 44-01242-604550
Email: ethics@gn.apc.org.

SRIs in the United States could do with some real competition in vegan-standard investment, and probably nothing would help more to bring about change than to get British firms like the EIG into the U.S. market. In the meantime, we've got to make do with what we've got; we can put our money where our hearts are by choosing SRIs which have the strongest animal rights criteria, while encouraging them along the animal rights road in whatever ways we can.

21

Common Concerns

People thinking about adopting a vegetarian diet are full of questions. Here are a few of the more common ones. I've modified the standard "Questions and Answers" format because I don't want to insult your intelligence by implying that I have *the* definitive answers. Rather, I give responses—information or perspectives that you might want to consider in coming to your own fuller understanding of vegetarianism, an understanding that fits you.

Question: *I don't feel satisfied when I don't eat meat. I feel hungry. Doesn't this mean I need meat?*

Response: No. *Any* dietary or other habit change can result in a less than satisfied feeling, as many travelers in other countries can attest. There are "icon foods" (often called "transition foods") that are especially useful for this problem—canned or frozen veggie-burgers or instant burger mix at health and natural food stores or through mail order. (With dry mixes, try adding tofu, grated carrots, chopped onions, etc., and tomato juice in place of the recommended water.) More natural protein foods such as tempeh, tofu, and wheat gluten are all excellent "meat substitutes." Most vegetarians use processed meat substitutes less frequently as their bodies get used to a more natural diet.

From the vegetarian perspective, try viewing meat as a substitute for plant protein, not the other way around. That was probably the case historically in many areas, with meat having been increasingly substituted for plant foods when climatic conditions forced the change.

Q: *What about eating out? Do I have to stay home when my meat-eating friends go out to a restaurant?*

R: Not at all. You won't have the variety of selection your friends have, but you certainly won't go hungry, either. Steak houses usually have salad bars, baked potatoes, and bean salad. Ethnic restaurants in cities often have vegetarian fare: the Middle Eastern falafel sandwich or hummus spread/dip, both made from high-protein garbanzo beans; meatless Italian pasta dishes; entire vegetarian menu sections in Indian restaurants; vegetable and tofu dishes in Chinese restaurants; and the good old all-American pizza, which vegans can order without cheese, though lard or mixed vegetable–animal shortening is sometimes used in making the pizza crust.

Don't be shy! Learn to ask waiters and waitresses what's vegetarian or vegan, and explain what you mean— no fish, fowl, or other meat, or meat derivatives; no milk products or eggs. You can also ask if the cook can prepare something for you on special order; it's often possible. If you wish, call the restaurant in advance, and/or let the people you're dining with know you're vegetarian. Such advance and detailed notice is absolutely essential, by the way, when you're invited to someone's house to eat. When you go to a potluck, you might want to take enough of your dish to satisfy you in case the other dishes have ingredients you don't want to eat. And try inviting your friends to a vegetarian restaurant!

Q: *What about kosher meats? Aren't they from animals that are raised naturally and killed humanely?*

R: Kosher meats are from animals raised like any other modern-day "food" animals; the difference is in the dying. One view of kosher laws is that they were originally, in part, an attempt to deal with humankind's having strayed from the vegetarian Garden of Eden, to give us at least a hint of sensitivity in our violent and barbaric ways. For example, if you were bound and determined to eat veal, at least you shouldn't add insult to injury by cooking the calf in his or her own mother's milk. The slaughter knife had to be as sharp as a scalpel to minimize the pain of the cut; animals couldn't be simply clubbed to death, as was apparently common in those days. And for health reasons (to keep people from selling corpses of animals who died of disease), kosher slaughter required that the animal be fully conscious when killed.

In modern slaughterhouses, with economic pressures for efficiency and profits, this means that animals experience the full terror of mechanized mass death, including very large, heavy animals being hoisted up by one leg for the throat slitting, often painfully dislocating joints in the process. Whether kosher slaughter is more cruel or less cruel than so-called "humane" nonkosher slaughter is beside the point—*any* slaughter is both cruel and unnecessary.

Those who feel kosher slaughter is more cruel may be disturbed to learn that, if they eat meat, they can't avoid kosher-slaughtered meat because a lot of it winds up being sold as nonkosher.

Kosher laws about food combining and utensil use all relate to animal foods; they are simply irrelevant in a total vegetarian diet. Veganism, then, is the ultimate kosher observance.

Q: *I'm already a vegetarian; I don't eat any red meat, only chicken and fish. Why should I give them up?*

R: Sorry to disappoint you, but chickens and fish are not vegetables. You'd never know it, though, by all the self-proclaimed "vegetarians" who simply abstain from what they call "red meat." Chickens bleed very red when killed, they're the most cruelly raised of all the "food" animals, and they're heavily drugged. Factory-farmed chickens live in their own and each others' feces while alive, and in mass automated slaughter the intestines sometimes get ripped open, spilling out the feces and contaminating the flesh with salmonella, which makes a lot of people sick with what may seem to be a "flu"; some even die. It's difficult to detect, given current inspection procedures, so don't expect the USDA to protect you. Time and again, random tests of packages of chicken meat in the supermarket find around a third of all samples to be infected with salmonella.

All animals, fish especially, concentrate toxic pollutants in their flesh. Even fish—the closest contender for vegetable status in some folks' minds—are often factory farmed like cows, pigs, and chickens. I read of one salmon-raising operation that kept the fish for life in underwater cages that frustrated their basic instinct to swim upstream and lay their eggs. The color of this factory-farmed salmon was reported as gray; wholesale buyers would point out on a color guide the color of flesh they wanted, and the fish farmer would add the right amount of the appropriate chemical to the water before killing the fish.

Fish are very sensitive creatures who suffer greatly when hooked or netted out of the water. (How would you feel in a fish's situation? Think about it.) The fishing industry is also the biggest killer of whales, dolphins, porpoises, turtles, and sea birds, who get entangled in fishing nets and drown. Whales need to come up for air sometimes, but can't when trapped in underwater nets. (Eat a fish, kill a whale.) And something like twenty pounds of "trash" fish are caught for every pound of the target species harvested.

Tuna drift nets used by huge fishing boats in the South Seas are called "walls of death" by the local islanders because they catch all species, including dolphins and even whales; the tuna are kept, and the rest are thrown away. The islanders' subsistence living through fishing is being destroyed by these big fishing fleets, while the Northeastern Atlantic fishing industries in the U.S. have collapsed, the fish populations decimated.

Q: *What about those fish oils I keep hearing about? Aren't they health promoting?*

R: There's a lot of unsubstantiated hype about fish oils. One of the claims, however, has some validity *if* you're a meat eater with a concomitant high risk of heart attack, the so-called "omega-3" fatty acids can apparently help reduce the risk of heart disease. But here's the catch that you don't get in the media hype: The omega-3s in fish and fish oil generate lots of free radicals, which, as discussed in chapter 7, are bad news. The *good* news is that there are omega-3s in plant foods, flaxseed oil being the richest source, and these are much more stable, meaning they don't produce so many free radicals. So, would you like your omega-3s with or without a large side order of free radicals?

What omega-3s are pretty good at doing is reducing somewhat the chance of heart attack by people who've placed themselves at high risk; if you're vegan, you've already dramatically reduced your risk.

The flap over omega-3s is just one of many examples of how we in a meat-eating culture use every new piece of scientific evidence as an excuse to continue our old ways and stay in denial about the damage we're doing. When one piece of evidence gets discredited, we grab onto the next new justification, until it gets discredited, and on and on. Just being aware of how we do this can help keep us from getting sidetracked from what we know is best for ourselves, for other creatures, and for the ecosystem.

Q: *Okay, so I go vegetarian, maybe vegan. How am I supposed to know if something has meat or other animal products in it?*

R: Ask, and read labels. Among the most common "hidden" meat products are gelatin (in marshmallows, Jell-O, some candies, etc.) and lard (in some pastries and in most refried beans, flour tortillas, and other Mexican foods). Many cheeses, including "natural" ones, are made with rennet, which comes from the stomach lining of a cow (some use a vegetable-based rennet). Vegans soon learn that there are milk and egg products in many pastries and breads. Whey, which comes from milk, is perhaps the sneakiest, and many of the supposedly nondairy soy cheeses contain casein or caseinates derived from cow's milk. Lactic acid is a slaughterhouse byproduct, and lactose is a milk sugar used in various foods including baked goods. Tallow and lard are animal fats. And then there's mono- and diglycerides, stabilizers, and emulsifiers which may have animal products. Sometimes, of course, you simply can't avoid such "sneaky meat." Just do the best you can.

Q: *Gee, with all these questions to ask and things to look out for, isn't it a big hassle being vegetarian, and especially vegan?*

R: It would be dishonest to say that being vegetarian, or especially vegan, is a breeze in our heavily carnivorous society. But compare it to the alternative—future disease, and living in conflict with your basic good intentions toward animals and the planet. The good news is that it's getting easier (almost by the day), as more and more people begin to understand the advantages of a plant-based diet and more and more vegetarian and vegan products arrive in the marketplace. When I moved to Europe in 1989, few Americans even knew what "vegan" meant—often even those working in vegetarian restaurants or natural food stores. On my return to the U.S. in 1993, that fact had changed; the local paper in the west coast town in which I'd settled would occasionally feature a human-interest or even front-page article using the word "vegan" without even bothering to explain it—the editors could safely assume that most readers would know what it meant. Mainstream advice columns offer advice to parents concerned that their kids have "gone vegan." The evolution toward veganism is reflected in the fact that in terms of social acceptance and attitudes, being vegan today is much like being vegetarian was in, say, the 1960s.

Q: *Wait a minute. My grandpa ate lots of meat and smoked like a chimney. He lived to be ninety-three, healthy and happy as a lark. So meat can't be all that bad, can it?*

R: Some people are born with stronger constitutions than others, and they can get away with more abuse to their bodies. The only way to learn the effects of various foods is to study a large group of people. Such studies clearly show that vegetarians are much healthier than meat eaters, and vegans even more so. Whatever your inherited strengths and weaknesses, you'll do better—greater health and more pleasure, less sickness and pain—on a plant-based diet.

Q: *But I know a vegetarian who looks really undernourished.*

R: That's very possible. There are several things to consider.

First, some vegetarians eat a "junk food" diet, with predictable consequences—bad health, an unstable personality, or both, the same as with nonvegetarian junk food junkies. Your friend may be one of those. Or she may have an unrelated digestion problem that inhibits the body's utilization of the food she eats. Or maybe she's just like a lot of us, who wait until we have a toothache before going to the dentist, or until we're physically or psychologically falling apart before making dietary and lifestyle changes.

Second, food is only one aspect of overall health; maybe your friend is neglecting herself in some other way.

Exercise, attitude, social connectedness, and other factors are also very important.

Third, be careful not to apply a double standard to vegetarians and nonvegetarians. For example, if a nonvegetarian gets sick, someone may assume it's because of a germ, stress, the weather, overwork, too much or too little sleep—you name it. But if a vegetarian, or especially a vegan, gets the same sickness, the diet is immediately suspect. It's irrational, but people tend to think that way about anything that's different from the social norm.

If you know vegans, vegetarians, and meat eaters, I think you'll easily notice the benefit of a plant-based diet. When I travel, I sometimes shop at supermarkets instead of natural food stores. In the checkout lines, I find it sad to notice the correlation between the varicose veins in women's legs and the amount of animal products in their shopping carts; repeated strained bowel movements caused by low-fiber diets (there's no dietary fiber in any animal product) destroys the one-way flow-control valves in the veins in the leg.

Q: *Shouldn't I ask my doctor before going vegetarian?*

R: Depends on the doctor. While a few are nutritionally enlightened, most are not so well informed; many are as culturally conditioned about food and nutrition as the general population. It wasn't long ago when medical conventions were smoky affairs, the M.D.s puffing away on cigarettes. While they've wised up in this way, at those same conventions the good doctors can still be seen feasting on rich, high-fat animal foods. Medical schools teach primarily diagnosis and the suppression of symptoms through drugs, radiation, and surgery (all of which in some cases can be valuable). The average medical student has only 2.5 hours of nutrition study during four years of school. While some medical schools are changing slowly, all too many doctors are still in the nutritional dark ages, and *thinking* they know it all only compounds their ignorance. When choosing a doctor, ask how much nutritional training they have, and what their view is of vegetarian, vegan, and animal-based diets.

Our idea of "doctor" is usually limited to allopathic doctors—M.D.s. In fact, allopaths so dominate health care in the U.S. that they don't even go by the term "allopath," they're just "doctors." Allopathy is great for some things like emergency treatment of traumatic injuries, life-threatening situations, surgery (though a lot of surgery is unnecessary or harmful, which is admitted in articles in medical journals from time to time), and suppressing or alleviating uncomfortable symptoms (often with means that also produce negative side effects). It also has some neat diagnostic tools, but when it comes to procedures and prescriptions, many feel it's guilty of overkill (so to speak).

Allopathy is only one of several branches of healing. In many countries, other forms of medicine are also popular, including herbal remedies, acupuncture, and naturopathy (which is based on the idea that the body's own healing power is the best medicine). Chiropractic has had to fight long and hard for marginal acceptance by allopaths; other modalities are still considered beyond the pale by mainstream M.D.s. But the times are changing. Each year, Americans make *several hundred million* visits to what allopaths call "alternative" practitioners, and a few allopaths are incorporating such approaches into their practice, or working together with alternative practitioners. Hippocrates, the father of medicine—who was himself *not* an allopath— would be pleased. (See Appendix C: Organizations for listing of "alternative" modalities.)

But don't fall into the trap of believing that just because someone is an "alternative" healer, she is competent, or even that all the assumptions on which her practice is based are valid.

Q: *Should I take supplements if I become a vegetarian? Don't I need to make up for vitamins and minerals I won't be getting in meat and animal products?*

R: With the possible exception of vitamin B-12, you're not going to "miss" anything good by giving up animal products, though you *will* miss a lot of things that undermine your health. And the animal foods take up space in your stomach that could be used for vegetables, fruits, beans, nuts, and grains, much richer sources of vital minerals and vitamins.

There are different opinions about supplements in general, whether for vegetarians or meat eaters. Some people say they're unnatural, that all necessary nutrition is contained in real foods, and that our concern about supplements is part of our indoctrination in a pill-popping culture. Others claim that in the modern condition of chemically grown foods transported over long distances and stored for long times, food values decrease, and therefore we need supplementation.

In addition, there is a wide range of biological variation from one person to another, and for any one of us, our nutritional needs can change from day to day, year to year. Pregnant women who are low in iron need to supplement during the second half of pregnancy, although supplementing when iron stores and supplies are adequate could lead to problems; if in doubt, get an iron test. Environmental and psychological factors—air and water quality, stress, and so on—also affect our need for various nutrients. To complicate things further, unusually large quantities of some nutrients can interfere with the absorption of others; a few can be toxic at doses that are too high.

The official Recommended Daily Allowance for various antioxidants like beta-carotene and vitamins A and E doesn't take into account the new information on their importance in keeping the immune system strong, slowing down the aging process, and preventing cancer.

A vegetable-rich diet, together with eliminating the fats that cause the free radicals in the first place, is good. If you're a junk food junkie, you might want to supplement with these antioxidants, but they're not a substitute for switching over to wholesome foods and exercise.

There is no one "correct" answer that is true for everyone all the time. Explore for yourself the arguments for and against supplements, and don't forget to listen to how your body feels. As with many things in life, you have to find what's right for you at a given time. Check a good medical source such as books from the Physicians Committee for Responsible Medicine (see Appendix C: Organizations).

Be aware that many supplements have ingredients or binders made of animal products, and labels usually won't tell you. Some brands have vegetarian lines, but the term "vegetarian," like the word "natural," has no legal definition, so you might want to look for more specific statements claiming "no animal products" and "no animal testing." If in doubt, you can write supplement companies with questions about their products; they usually respond. You may also obtain pure, cruelty-free supplements from humane suppliers (see Appendix D: Cruelty Free Products).

Q: *My vegan friend doesn't use silk or honey. Why?*

R: Silkworms are boiled alive in their cocoons to keep them from cutting their way out and thereby destroying the continuous silk thread. In collecting honey, there's no way to know that the beekeeper left enough for the bees' use, and even careful collectors sometimes accidentally crush bees or break off their wings while collecting the honey. Some beekeepers find it's more economical to simply smoke or burn the adult bees to death at the end of the season and grow a new "crop" from the remaining eggs. Finally, for the production of new queen bees, artificial insemination is now the norm. According to the Vegan-L Internet mailing list, "the favored method of obtaining bee sperm is by pulling off the [male] insect's head. Decapitation sends an electrical impulse to the nervous system which causes sexual arousal. The lower half of the headless bee is then squeezed to make it ejaculate. The resulting liquid is collected in a hypodermic syringe."

Q: *What else does being a vegan involve?*

R: People who go vegan at least in part for ethical reasons having to do with the suffering of other creatures try to avoid all animal products for the same reason they avoid milk, eggs, and meat. For example, leather is not just a byproduct; buying it contributes to the overall economic demand for factory farming and slaughterhouses. Sheep are specially bred to produce more wool than is good for them. After multiple shearings—leaving them with *less* than what they need—they are killed for their meat. Eighty percent of U.S. wool comes from Australia. Millions die on outback farms, and twice as many in transport to ritual slaughter in the Middle East. A substantial part of the wool on the market is "skin wool" taken from the skins of slaughtered sheep and lambs, or those who die from exposure, neglect, or disease.

Uncountable numbers of insects are raised to be killed to make cochineal, a red coloring used in foods and clothing, while the crushed wings of others are used in making iridescent eye shadow. White sugar is generally filtered through charcoal made from animal bones. Wine may be clarified using edible gelatins (made from bones), isinglass (made from the swim bladders of fish), casein and potassium caseinate (milk proteins), or animal albumin (egg albumin and dried blood powder), according to Vegan-L.

At least two European vegan societies publish lists of domestic and imported *organic* wines that are vegan; most organic wines don't make the list, and some aren't even vegetarian. So far, no one has taken a close look at

American and imported wines, organic or otherwise, from a vegetarian or vegan perspective. You can write your favorite organic wine company and ask. Apparently kosher wines are vegan (as are kosher marshmallows; regular ones are made from gelatin). Some beer uses isinglass as a clarifier, and some vodkas are passed through charcoal made from animal bones.

Q: *What about down?*

R: A lot of down these days comes from abroad, from countries like China. Practices vary from country to country, region to region. "Lucky" birds are killed and then plucked. The unlucky ones are "live plucked," in other words, they have their feathers ripped out several times during their short lives. These repeated "gatherings" begin when the geese are about eight weeks old and end when the birds are finally slaughtered. For sleeping bags and winter jackets, there are now very good synthetic alternatives to this not-so-natural material.

Q: *If I go vegan, what about the calcium in milk? I'll be missing one of the basic food groups!*

R: For all of recorded history up until only a few decades ago, there were no "food groups." People intuitively sought in their environment the foods that provided what their bodies needed. Depending on environmental conditions, they got their calcium from any of a number of sources: milk; whole, unhulled (brown) sesame seeds (most of the calcium is in the hull); kelp and other sea vegetables, including agar (vegetarian "gelatin"); and soybeans, almonds, and dark green leafy vegetables (especially kale, turnip greens, and collards). All are rich in calcium. There are also other factors like exercise, which helps us assimilate calcium, and sugar and caffeine, which cause calcium loss.

Knowledge is power, and nutritional science can help us improve our diets and health. Calcium is a nutrient that, like protein, performs many essential tasks in the body.

When a deficiency occurs, it is usually not because of inadequate dietary intake, but because of other factors such as excessive protein intake and eating foods too high in phosphorous in relation to calcium. Meats are especially bad in both of these regards.

Excess protein results in the leaching of calcium from the body; a lower but adequate level of protein means that less calcium is needed in the diet, because then we retain more of our calcium stores. A vegan diet that includes such calcium-rich vegetables as mustard and turnip greens, dandelion greens, collards, kale, and romaine and loose-leaf lettuce easily meets our calcium needs. What we have to be careful of is to not get *too much* calcium, which also contributes to calcium kidney stones, or too much protein, which in turn leaches calcium from the bones and teeth. Osteoporosis plagues meat and dairy eaters but is almost unknown in basically vegan cultures.

It's important to remember that the old four food groups were set up under the watchful eye and weighty political influence of the interconnected meat, egg, and milk industries, which to this day provide free promotional ("educational") literature to schools, including lesson plans rather shamelessly promoting their products. Luckily, we now have the New Four Food Groups to guide our food choices.

Q: *Don't plants feel pain when they're killed for us to eat?*

R: Actually, while plants are alive and should be treated with thoughtfulness and respect, there is no consensus, even among vegetarians, on whether they feel pain, or what pain might mean for them. "But what about plants?" is a completely valid question which some people misuse to keep from facing the reality of what happens to highly sentient (feeling) "food" animals.

Regardless of our view of plants, most of us can agree that animals have a good deal in common with us physiologically, and feel physical and emotional pain much as we do—

in some cases, more intensely. Both science and common experience show they suffer. I myself have hunted and gardened. While both involve violence to other life forms, on an experiential gut level, pulling a carrot out of the ground or trimming a fruit tree seems less violent than slitting the throat of an animal. The violence that we do to others is psychological violence to ourselves. In other words, I have to desensitize myself more to kill animals than to garden, something not easily seen by people who live their whole lives without actually killing any of the animals (or plants) that they eat. For those of us who do kill what we eat, once we're desensitized in any area of our lives, it becomes difficult for us to see our desensitization. It becomes our normal condition.

But even if plants are highly sensitive to pain, or even if you believe that they are *more* sensitive than animals, the vegetarian argument holds firm. Because plants are fed to "food" animals, a far greater number of plants is required to produce meat, milk, and eggs than to provide our nutrition needs directly. If plants feel pain and fear, as some research indicates and as some people instinctively feel, it seems to be in a more generalized, less sharp way, though we can't know for sure. But, in any case, we cause the death of a lot more plants when we eat animal products than when we eat plants directly. A plant-based diet greatly reduces the number of plants killed in order for us to live.

Q: *But what about spirit? The spirit in animals is the same as the spirit in plants, so there's no difference in killing a plant or an animal to eat.*

R: There is also spirit in humans, but we don't kill humans to eat. It's not a question of whether something has spirit or a soul—something that philosophers and theologians have debated inconclusively for centuries. Rather, it's a matter of whether suffering results from our actions or how much suffering it causes and how necessary it is. Fish, birds, and mammals have highly developed nervous systems and feel physical pain; many also feel emotional pain (fear, dread, sadness) when facing imminent death or when separated from their offspring or other loved ones. The clincher is that it's not at all necessary for us to cause this pain.

A friend raised in a monastery once told me that theologians—males—convened in the Middle Ages to decide whether women and animals had souls. After much discussion, a vote was taken; women squeaked by and got souls, while animals lost the vote and went soulless.

Spiritual development is full of pitfalls. One is that egos are extremely clever, and can take something that's true, twist it, and use it as a rationalization for unnecessary violence or for passivity in the face of injustice. This is an especially dangerous pitfall for those of us who are insulated by money, family, friends, physical distance, or privileged human status from such reality checks as the sights, sounds, and smells of factory farms and slaughterhouses.

Q: *But if everybody became vegetarian, and especially vegan, what would happen to the animals?*

R: Not everyone is going to make the switch all at once; it's a gradual process, with the numbers growing day by day, year by year. Food animals don't mate, they're "bred" at the decisions of their human masters. When demand for animal products goes up, they're bred more; when it goes down, they're bred less. As the consumption of animal products declines, so will the population of captive food animals, through less breeding.

Or, to answer your question in a different way, if everybody became vegan, then we'd be able to stop exploiting animals and begin to see and treat them as the marvelous beings that they are.

Q: *So what about my pets? Cats and dogs are carnivores, so I guess I'll have to continue to feed them meat, right?*

R: Not any more. Actually, dogs are omnivores and can do well on a nonmeat diet, though some will rebel at first to the switch. With cats it's trickier. They're carnivores, and need taurine in their diet; taurine occurs primarily in animal flesh. Without it, cats can go blind or develop heart disease. But several companies now sell vegetarian and even vegan dog and cat food with synthesized taurine, and one company manufactures and sells a supplement called Vegepet that you just add to the food that you feed your companion animal (sample recipes are included with the supplement). This is a lot more natural than the chemicals that go into cat and dog food. The supplements are available for both cats and dogs, with mixes of nutrients (vitamins A and C, enzymes, etc.) appropriate to various stages of their life cycles. There's a book on the subject, and a toll-free number for orders (see Appendix D: Cruelty-Free Products).

Q: *I think I can give up eating eggs and cheese and drinking milk, but what about baking? What about all those yummy baked goods?*

R: Milk products are easily eliminated from most recipes, or replaced with soy milk, tahini (sesame butter) and water, or cashew milk made by blending raw cashews and water together. Eggs can also be simply left out of a number of baked goods with no problem. In baked goods, eggs help with rising or binding, or provide moistness. You can get an egg replacer (check to make sure it's vegan) or make your own. For leavening, you can use extra baking soda or baking powder without aluminum. Moistness can be increased by adding water, fruit juice, applesauce, mashed banana, or a little oil. In short, where there's a will, there's a way.

The FAQ (Frequently Asked Questions list) from Vegan-L, the vegan mailing list (a sort of forum) on the Internet suggests these equivalents for one egg: 2 oz. of soft tofu blended with some water (for consistency); 2 oz. of mashed beans, mashed potatoes, or nut butters; 1/2 mashed banana; 1/4 cup applesauce or pureed fruit; one tablespoon flax seeds (found in natural food stores) with 3 tablespoons water, blended for two to three minutes, or boiled for ten minutes or until desired consistency is achieved; or 1 teaspoon soy flour plus 1 tablespoon water. Arrowroot or kudzu root powder and tapioca are also used as egg replacers.

Q: *OK, I'm convinced, except for one thing. I'd like to go vegan, not just vegetarian. But doesn't vitamin B-12 occur only in animal products? Don't we need B-12?*

R: B-12 is a vitamin essential to health, and a deficiency can lead to pernicious anemia (B-12 deficiency disease) and eventual degeneration of the nervous system. We're talking very serious stuff here.

B-12 is made by microorganisms in the soil and water. In the old days, a vegan might well have gotten all the B-12 she needed from the surface of root vegetables and by drinking water. But with increasing chemical pollution of soil and water, many of these microorganisms have been killed off. Since animals get their B-12 from the soil and water, too, even meat today has less B-12 than it used to.

All animal products, including milk and eggs but especially red meat, contain B-12. Both the whites and the yolks of eggs seem to *block* B-12 absorption, and chicken and fish are poor sources of the vitamin.

The vitamin is also manufactured in the small intestines; the only question is whether our bodies make enough of it and absorb it. Chlorella and various cultured soy foods contain the vitamin, as does, reportedly, at least some blue-green algae, though the quantities can be extremely small and these forms of B-12 may not absorb well into the body.

This whole subject is somewhat controversial in vegetarian circles. Most vegans like myself go the conservative route by occasionally taking supplemental B-12 derived from a natural fermentative process. Unlike with calcium and protein, there is no evidence that even very high B-12 intake is harmful, and supplements are apparently absorbed well in the body. There is some evidence that high intake of vitamin C and other vitamins *may* interfere with B-12 metabolism, so if you take a *lot* of vitamin C you might want to take B-12, too. Since cooking partly destroys B-12, meat eaters might want to eat meat bloody raw the natural way, maybe biting it directly off the cow for maximum freshness—if it weren't for those nagging concerns about animal suffering, and if it weren't for the problem of disease transmission from animals to humans.

The Recommended Daily Allowance for vitamin B-12 has been set at far above most people's actual need, at two millionths of a gram (2.0 micrograms) per day. So a tiny 50-microgram dose will cover you for almost a month. There are few cases in the medical literature of B-12 deficiency disease (pernicious anemia) due to inadequate dietary intake. The relatively rare deficiency cases that occur are usually due to an inability to metabolize the vitamin, and most cases occur with nonvegetarians. For someone with an impaired ability to metabolize B-12, having extra in the diet could make the difference between being healthy and developing serious health problems.

Excess amounts (which all meat eaters have) are stored in the body at least two years, so relax. Give your kid natural B-12 supplements occasionally until he's old enough to make his own decisions; you don't have a right to gamble with his health, and vegan B-12 supplements are made by a natural process. For yourself, you have at least two years' supply in your body, but just to give yourself peace of mind, take a natural supplement every month or so, read and discuss a variety of opinions on the subject, and then decide for yourself.

After all, isn't that part of what your step into vegetarianism is all about—taking charge of your decisions, your health, your life?

22

In a Nutshell

You and I want to love and be loved, to care and be cared for; we really don't want to hurt, or violate, or kill. We used to believe that we had to do that to live; we were trained to accept violence as normal.

Now we know there are alternatives. Now we can leave behind our inherited patterns of violence and domination, creating together a better world for all beings.

There are lots of very good reasons for going vegetarian and vegan, ranging from health to ecology, from helping alleviate world hunger to being kind to animals, from personal growth to moral integrity, sweeter kisses, and better sex.

On the other hand, except for people in extenuating conditions such as arctic cold, arid desert, war, or famine, there are only four reasons *not* to make the change: **habit** (including our conditioned tastes), **ignorance** (about the impacts of our choices on ourselves and others, and about alternatives), **fear** (of ridicule, or of change itself), and **indifference to suffering** (calluses on our souls).

It's as simple as that.

I used to feel I needed to hunt to be a man. I thought I had to eat meat, cheese, and eggs to be healthy. I was afraid to change my eating patterns, I was afraid to be different. So I know well the power of habit, ignorance, and fear—and the doubt and apprehension that can accompany a major change. I also know that change is possible, that there's pleasure in the transition, and that so much more awaits us on the other side than we "give up" in the crossing.

This book is an invitation for you to embark on that journey, or to continue and expand on it, in whatever ways are most appropriate for the strong, caring person that you are.

Welcome to the revolution.

DataBank

Appendix A:
Further Information

The following is a sampling of what's available. Check your local natural food store or bookstore for these and other titles. Write the North American Vegetarian Society, the American Vegan Society, the Vegetarian Resource Group, *Vegetarian Times* magazine, and other sources listed in this DataBank for mail order lists.

In addition, the Book Publishing Company (800-695-2241) has a free catalog with nice illustrations and explanations of various vegetarian and vegan books and cookbooks, books on Native American subjects, natural and nontoxic cleaning, humane pest control, etc. Health book distributor Dennis Nelson offers an extensive selection of vegan cookbooks; for his Catalog for Healthful Living, with small photos of the book covers, send $3 (applicable toward first order) to P.O. Box 2302, Santa Cruz, CA 95063. Other organizations sell a more limited selection of specialized books in their field, e.g., health and medical books from Physicians Committee for Responsible Medicine. Compare titles and prices on various lists. See Appendix C: Organizations for addresses and phone numbers not given here.

Following the main listing below are separate categories for Books and Publications: Other Languages; Software; Birthing, Babies and Kids; Religion and Spirituality; Audio-Visual/Media; and Periodicals.

Additives You Need to Know About, by Beatrice Trum Hunter.

Ahimsa, by Nathaniel Altman. Theosophical Publishing House, 1980. Nonviolence in eating and living.

Alternative Medicine Yellow Pages and *Alternative Medicine: The Definitive Guide.* Future Publishing, 5009 Pacific Hwy. E., Suite 6, Fife, WA 98424. Orders: 800-720-6363.

Animal Factories, by Jim Mason and Peter Singer. "The mass production of animals for food and how it affects the lives of consumers, farmers, and the animals themselves."

Animal Ingredients and their Alternatives, by Nermin Buyukmihci and D. Carol Watson. A good reference for avoiding less obvious animal products.

Animal Liberation: A Graphic Guide, by Lori Gruen, Peter Singer, and David Hine. Camden Press, London, 1987.

Animal Liberation: A New Ethic for Our Treatment of Animals, by Peter Singer. Random House, 1990. Also available in Spanish (see Other Languages section below).

Animals, Property and the Law, by Gary Francione. Especially for lawyers, philosophers, and ethicists. Temple University Press, 1995. Foreword by William Kunster.

Become a Vegetarian in Five Easy Steps, by Christine Beard, McBooks, 1996.

Beyond beef: The Rise & Fall of the Cattle Culture, by Jeremy Rifkin. NAL Dutton, 1992.

Building the Green Movement, by Rudolf Bahro. New Society Publishers, 1986. Papers by Bahro, former theorist of Die Grünen (the German Greens) and radical ecologist, on the fundamental crisis of industrial society and western civilization, including human treatment of animals.

Choices for Our Future: A Generation Rising for Life on Earth, by Ocean Robbins and Sol Solomon, two founders of Youth for Environmental Sanity (YES!). Inspiring and irreverent.

Clean Your House Safely and Effectively without Harmful Chemicals, by Randy Dunford. Book Publishing Company, 1993.

Compassion: The Ultimate Ethic, by Victoria Moran. An exploration of veganism. Nutrition, ecology, children, weight reduction, recipes for vegan "milks," "cheeses," "ice creams," etc.

Composition and Facts about Food, by Ford Heritage. Reference. Mokelumne Hill Press, 1968. Ring bound.

Conscientious Objectors, by Gary L. Francione and Anne E. Charlton. About dissection and vivisection as classroom procedures only. Available from the American Anti-Vivisection Society, 801 Old York Road, #204, Jenkintown, PA 19046-1685; tel: 215-887-0816; fax: 215-887-2088.

Co-op America's National Green Pages. Co-op America foundation, annual. 1400 companies selling things from housewares and furniture to clothing and art supplies, cleaning and architectural services, vegetarian book publishers, and nonviolent toys. Orders: 800-584-7336.

Despair and Personal Power in the Nuclear Age, by Joanna Rogers Macy. New Society Publishers, 1983.

Dick Gregory's Natural Diet for Folks Who Eat: Cooking with Mother Nature, by Dick Gregory. Harper Perennial, 1973.

Diet for a New America, by John Robbins. Stillpoint Publishing. A classic.

Dr. Dean Ornish's Program for Reversing Heart Disease, by Dean Ornish, M.D. Ballantine, 1992.

The Dreaded Comparison: Human and Animal Slavery, by Marjorie Spiegel. New Mirror Books, 1989 (2nd edition). Available from New Society Publishers.

Eat Right, Live Longer, by Neal Barnard, M.D. Physicians Committee for Responsible Medicine. Crown, 1995.

European Vegetarian Guide: Restaurants and Hotels. Hans-Nietsch-Verlag, 1993. German, English, and French.

The Extended Circle: A Dictionary of Humane Thought, edited by Jon Wynne-Tyson. Cardinal, 1990. Available from American Vegan Society. Quotes from persons famous and common.

Famous Vegetarians and their Favorite Recipes, by Ryan Berry. Pythagorean Books, 1994.

Food for Life: How the New Four Food Groups Can Save Your Life, by Neal Barnard, M.D. Crown, 1993. Includes recipes and menus.

Healthy School Lunch Action Guide, by Susan Campbell and Todd Winant. EarthSave, 1995. How to get vegan meal alternatives in your child's school lunch program.

The Heretic's Feast: A History of Vegetaianism, by Colin Spencer. University Press of New England, 1995.

Least Toxic Home Pest Control by Dan Stein. Book Publishing Company, 1994. Outsmart pests instead of killing them.

The Love-Powered Diet: When Willpower Is Not Enough, by Victoria Moran. New World Library, 1993.

May All Be Fed: Diet for a New World, by John Robbins. William Morrow, 1992. Philosophy, politics, and 175 excellent recipes.

McDougall's Medicine, by John McDougall, M.D., and Mary McDougall. New Win Publishing, 1986. With recipes.

Meatless Meals for the Working Person, by Debra Wasserman and Charles Stahler. Vegetarian Resource Group, 1994.

A Natural Education: Native American Ideas and Thoughts, compiled by Stan Padilla. Book Publishing Company, 1994.

New Realities for the '90s, excerpted from *Diet for a New America,* by John Robbins. A sixteen-page booklet of concentrated facts. Quantity discounts.

Not Tested on Animals, from People for the Ethical Treatment of Animals. Updated annually. Also indicates which products are vegan (containing no animal products). An abbreviated list is available from PETA for free.

Nutrition for Vegetarians, by Agatha Thrash, M.D., and Calvin Thrash, Jr., M.D. New Lifestyles Books, 1982. Nutritional information.

Peter Burwash's Vegetarian Primer, by Peter Burwash and John Tullius. Athenium, 1983.

A Physician's Slimming Guide, by Neal Barnard, M.D. Book Publishing Company, 1992.

The Politics of Nonviolent Action, by Gene Sharp. Three volumes. Porter Sargent Publishers, 1974. Nonviolent ways to defend a society; not about diet or vegetarianism.

Power of the People: Active Nonviolence in the United States, by Robert Cooney and Helen Michalowski. New Society Publishers, 1987. A written and pictorial history.

The Power of Your Plate, by Neal Barnard, M.D. Book Publishing Company, 1995.

Radical Vegetarianism: A Dialectic of Diet and Ethic, by Mark M. Braunstein. Panacea Press, 1993 (2nd edition).

The Right Bite, school teachers' nutritional information kit from Physicians Committee for Responsible Medicine; includes masters for photocopying.

The Sexual Politics of Meat: A Feminist-Vegetarian Critical Theory, by Carol J. Adams. Continuum, 1990 (cloth), 1991 (paper). Parallels between the oppression of women and the victimization of other-than-human animals. An Internet mailing list exists solely for discussion of this book (see Appendix H: Vegetarian Online Resources).

The Simple Soybean and Your Health, by Mark Messina and Virginia Messina. Avery, 1994.

A Teen's Guide to Going Vegetarian, by Judy Krizmanic. Penguin/Puffin Books, 1994.

The Tofu Tollbooth, by Dar Williams. Ardwork Press, 1994. A directory of natural food stores in the U.S. Credit card orders: 800-863-8246.

The Vegan Cookbook, by Alan Wakeman and Gordon Baskerville. Faber & Faber, 1986.

Vegan Nutrition: A Survey of Research, by Gill Langley. The Vegan Society (U.K.), 1995 (2nd edition includes new large section on "Vegan Mothers and Children").

Vegan Nutrition: Pure and Simple, by Michael Klaper, M.D. Gentle World, 1987. Includes recipes.

Vegan Passport, published by the Vegan Society (U.K.), 1996. Written statements in the native script of many of the world's languages stating that you're vegan, what that means, and examples of foods in the specific culture that you do and don't eat. An invaluable travel resource. Available starting Spring 1996 from the Vegan Society (U.K.) or the American Vegan Society (see Appendix C: Organizations). [Note: the predecessor to this book, *Vegetarian Passport,* from the Nederlandse Vegetariersbond (Dutch Vegetarian Society), is no longer in print.]

Veganic Gardening: The Alternative System for Healthier Crops, by Kenneth Dalziel O'Brien. Thorsons, 1986.

Vegetarian Asia: A Travel Guide, by Teresa Bergen, Noble Poodle Press,1994. P.O. Box 641188, San Francisco, CA 94109.

Vegetarian Cats and Dogs, by James Peden. Harbingers for a New Age, 717 E. Missoula Ave., Troy, MT 59935-9609; 1995 (2nd edition). Tel.: 800-884-6262. Solution to the moral quandary of ethical vegetarians and vegans who have companion animals.

Vegetarian Handbook. Toronto Vegetarian Society, 1994. Restaurant, shopping, and travel guide available for both Toronto-only and Canada-wide editions.

Vegetarian Journal's Guide to Natural Foods Restaurants in the U.S. and Canada. Avery, 1994 (2nd edition).

The Vegetarian's Self-Defense Manual, by Richard Bargen, M.D. Theosophical Publishing House, 1979.

A Vegetarian Sourcebook: The Nutrition, Ecology, and Ethics of a Natural Foods Diet, by Keith Akers. Vegetarian Press, 1989 (3rd edition).

Vegetarianism: A Way of Life, by Dudley Giehl. Barnes & Noble, 1981.

What Are We Feeding Our Kids? by Michael F. Jacobson. Workman Publishing Company, 1994.

Other Languages

European Vegetarian Guide: Restaurants and Hotels. Hans-Nietsch-Verslag, 1993. In German, English, and French.

"La Corrida de Toros." Disponible por People for the Ethical Treatment of Animals. Pamphlet.

Liberación Animal: Una Etica Nueva para Nuestro Trato hacia los Animales, por Peter Singer. Asociación de Lucha para Evitar la Crueldad con los Animales, A.C., Apdo. Postal 105-58, 11580 México 5, D.F., Mexico. Disponible por People for the Ethical Treatment of Animals.

"There's No Excuse"/"Es inexcusable," anti-fur leaflet in nine languages: German, Italian, French, English, Dutch, Russian, Japanese, Spanish, and Swedish. People for the Ethical Treatment of Animals.

"Una Dieta Vegetariana." Disponible por Vegetarian Resource Group. Tri-fold pamphlet.

Software

The Vegetarian Game, IBM-compatible software. Vegetarian Resource Group.

"Vegie Card," Hyperstack program for Macintosh. EarthSave. All aspects of vegetarianism. Freeware, copying encouraged. $6 + $3 shipping for floppy.

Birthing, Babies, and Kids

The Complete Guide and Cookbook for Raising Your Child as a Vegetarian, by Michael and Nina Shandler. Ballantine, 1982.

Convert-A-Parent. One of 12 brochures/booklets on "how to deal with patronising, aggressive, stupid, ignorant school friends, how to put your family completely at ease, and best of all, how to finally turn them into totally committed vegetarians and vegans," available for donation and/or international postal reply coupon from Vegetarians International Voice for Animals (Viva!), P.O. Box 212, Crewe, CW1 4SD, UK. Tel: +44-1270-522500, Fax: +44-1270-522511.

Eat Smart: A Guide to Good Health for Kids, by Dale Figtree. New Win Publishing, 1992. For young people. Illustrated.

The Experience of Childbirth, by Sheila Kitzinger. Viking Penguin, 1990.

Feeding Vegan Babies, by Freya Dinshah. American Vegan Society.

I Love Animals and Broccoli: A Children's Activity Book, by Debra Wasserman and Charles Stahler. Vegetarian Resource Group, 1995.

Leprechaun Cake and Other Tales: A Vegetarian Story-Cookbook, by Debra Wasserman. Vegetarian Resource Group, 1995.

Nature's Chicken: The Story of Today's Chicken Farms, by Nigel Burroughs. Book Publishing Company, 1992. Whimsical, somewhat humorous way to teach/learn compassion.

Pregnancy, Children, and the Vegan Diet, by Michael Klaper, M.D. Gentle World, 1988. Includes recipes.

Raising Your Family Naturally (formerly *The Vegetarian Child*), by Joy Gross. Carol Publishing Group, 1988. Not vegan.

The Soup to Nuts Natural Foods Coloring Book, by Ellen Sue Spivak.

Vegan Nutrition, by Gill Langley. Vegan Society (U.K.), 1995. Large new section on "Vegan Mothers and Children."

Vegetarian Baby, by Sharon Yntema. McBooks Press, 1980. Short section on vegan diets.

Vegetarian Children, by Sharon Yntema. McBooks Press, 1987. Short section on vegan diets.

The Vegetarian Mother Baby Book, by Rose Elliot. Pantheon books, 1986.

Vegetarian Pregnancy: The Definitive Nutritional Guide to Having a Healthy Baby, by Sharon Yntema. McBooks Press, 1994.

The Whale's Tale, by Deborah Evans Smith. Sea Fog Press, 1987. For young children. A whale saves a whaling ship from a storm.

What's Wrong with Eating Meat? by Polefka. Book Publishing Company. For teaching children about meat.

Religion and Spirituality

Several Jewish publications are available from Micah Publications, 255 Humphrey Street, Marblehead, MA 01945, or from Jewish Vegetarians of North America (see Appendix C: Organizations).

Animals and Christianity: A Book of Readings, edited by Andrew Linzey and Tom Regan. Crossroad Publishing, 1990.

Christianity and the Rights of Animals, by Andrew Linzey. Crossroad Publishing, 1987.

Creation Spirituality by Matthew Fox. Harper San Francisco, 1991. Not about vegetarianism. (Also *Original Blessing* by Matthew Fox).

Devout Vegetarians, by Rynn Berry.

Food for the Gods: Vegetarianism and the World Religions, by Ryan Berry. Pythagorean Books, 1996. Interviews with vegetarian representatives of the world religions, with vegan recipes from each religion.

Food for the Spirit: Vegetarianism and the World Religions, by Steven Rosen. Bala Books, 1987.

Haggadah for the Vegetarian Family: An Egalitarian Traditional Service, by Roberta Kalechofsky. Micah Publications, 1993.

Inroads. A newsletter of the International Network for Religion and Animals, P.O. Box 1335, North Wales, PA 19454-0335.

Jewish Vegetarian Year. A calendar. Available from Micah Publications.

Judaism and Vegetarianism, by Richard Schwartz. Micah Publications, 1988. History, scripture, recipes, menus, organizations, arguments. Not vegan.

To Cherish All Life: A Buddhist Case for Becoming Vegetarian, by Roshi Philip Kapleau. The Zen Center, 1981.

Tree of Life: Buddhism and Protection of Nature, by Nancy Nash. Buddist Perception of Nature, 1987. English, Tibetan, and Thai.

We Are All Noah (film and videocassette). See Audio-Visual/Media, below.

Audio-Visual/Media

Organizations listed after title indicates either the producer or one of perhaps several sources the video is available from. Unless noted otherwise, the listing is a VHS video.

The Animals Film. A 2 hr. and 15 min. film or videocassette on all areas of animal abuse. The Cinema Guild, 1697 Broadway, New York, NY 10019. Tel: 212-246-5522.

A Diet for All Reasons, by Michael Klaper, M.D. Vegan. EarthSave.

Diet for a New America: The Documentary. A 60-min. PBS video hosted by John Robbins, with a variety of experts. Introduction to the effects of the American meat-based diet. EarthSave.

Fit For Life, Sunrise Productions. 52 min. Food prep demos by Marilyn Diamond. From Farm Animal Reform Movement.

Food For Thought. A 30-min. exposé of environmental damages by animal agriculture.

Friendly Foods: Gourmet Vegetarian Cuisine, by Brother Ron Pickarski. Step-by-step cooking training.

Healthy School Lunch Program, A 4-min. video shows the impact of the Healthy School Lunch Program. EarthSave.

Healthy, Wealthy, and Wise. A 30-min. intro to vegetarian lifestyles. Farm Animals Reform Movement.

Live Longer, Live Better. Audio cassette by Neal Barnard, M.D. 1992. Physicians Committee for Responsible Medicine.

Marilyn Diamond's Fit for Life Kitchen. Domino Productions, 1990. Includes recipe booklet for the nine entrees demonstrated.

The McDougall Video, by John McDougall, M.D. *Lifestyle Magazine,* 1994. Best segments from "McDougall's Medicine" TV series.

Truth or Dairy. Narrated by British Rastafarian poet Benjamin Zephaniah, The Vegan Society (U.K.), 1994. Available from the American Vegan Society in U.S. video format. See chapter 13, "The Vegan Alternative", for more on this video. Approximately 20 min. Upbeat.

Vegetarian World. A 30-min. film or videocassette with William Shatner (of Star Trek fame). Bullfrog films, 1984.

We Are All Noah, The Culture and Animals Foundation, 3509 Eden Croft Drive, Raleigh, NC 27612. Telephone: 919-782-3739. 1986. 28-min., on food and lab animals and human obligations toward animals in the Judeo-Christian tradition.

Your Diet and Future of Life: The Windsor Video, John Robbins. EarthSave.

Periodicals

Ahimsa, published by the American Vegan Society.

The Animals' Agenda, "Helping People Help Animals." Bimonthly, dedicated to informing people about animal rights and cruelty-free living, and fostering greater cooperation between animal-advocate individuals and organizations. Subscriptions: 800-825-0061. Editorial address: P.O. Box 25881, Baltimore, MD 21224. Tel: 410-675-4566; Fax: 410-675-0066; email: 75543.3331@compuserve.com.

The Animals' Voice. Animal rights magazine with a lot of glossy color photos, and *The Activists' Voice* newsletter (each published quarterly). P.O. Box 16955, North Hollywood, CA 91615-9931. Tel: 800-828-6423; Fax: 818-883-3729.

Good Medicine. Publication of Physicians Committee for Responsible Medicine, P.O. Box 6322, Washington, D.C. 20015. Tel: 202-686-2210. Nutrition, psychology of changing habits, and lowfat, cholesterol-free, non-animal recipes. Subscription with membership. PCRM also produces "The Right Bite," curriculum guide for use by classroom teachers.

Green Horizon. Green Politics Network, RFD 2, Box 3292, Bowdoinham, ME 04008. About Green politics, not vegetarianism. Send SASE for current subscription prices and to ask about any new national Green publications.

Health Science. A monthly magazine of the American Natural Hygiene Society, 12816 Race Track Road, Tampa, FL 33625. Fasting, raw food, health. Subscriptions: 800-666-8576, includes membership.

How On Earth! magazine, Box 339, Oxford PA 19363. Tel: 717-529-8638, Fax: 717-529-2000, email: howonearth@aol.com or howonearth@igc.apc.org. Published quarterly. Send SASE for info.

Inroads. The newsletter of the International Network for Religion and Animals. See Religion and Spirituality, this appendix.

Natural Health, monthly magazine of macrobiotics and natural living. Editorial: 17 Station Street, Box 1200, Brookline, MA 02147. Subscriptions: 800-666-8576.

Vegetarian Journal, published quarterly in magazine format by the Vegetarian Resource Group, P.O. Box 1463, Baltimore, MD 21203. Tel: 410-366-VEGE (8343); email: bobbi@clark.net. Does not accept advertising, so as to remain editorially free of commercial influence. Recipes, articles, reviews.

Vegetarian Times, national vegetarian magazine. Recipes, human interest features, and news items on a variety of diet-related subjects, with an emphasis on health. P.O. Box 570, Oak Park, IL 60303. Tel (editorial): 708-848-8100; fax: 708-848-8175. Subscriptions and mail order: 800-435-9610.

Veggie Life. "Growing, cooking, eating green." Box 412, Mt. Morris, IL 61054-8163. Tel: 510-671-9852.

DataBank

Appendix B:
Recipe Books and Cookbooks

The following is a list of many of the recipe books coming out in the last few years. I have attempted to include only titles which are all or mostly vegan, except in specialized interest areas (child raising, religion). Because new titles are appearing all the time and prices change, specific ordering information for each book is not given. Ask your local bookstore to order, or write the mail-order places listed in the introductory paragraph of Appendix A.

This appendix is titled "Recipe Books and Cookbooks" because not all books on how to prepare food involve cooking (e.g., *The Joy of Not Cooking,* below).

The Almost No-Fat Cookbook, by Bryanna Clark Grogan. Book Publishing Company, 1994.

The American Vegetarian Cookbook, by Marilyn Diamond, coauthor of the bestseller *Fit for Life.* Warner Books, 1990.

The Book of Miso, (Ten Speed Press, 1983), *The Book of Tempeh,* (Soyfoods Center, 1980), *The Book of Tofu,*

(Ballantine, 1987), and many other titles by William Shurtleff and Akiko Aoyagi. How to make and use these soy foods.

Burgers 'n Fries 'n Cinnamon Buns: Low-Fat Meatless Versions of Fast Food Favorites, by Bobbie Hinman. Book Publishing Company, 1993.

The Compassionate Cook, by People for the Ethical Treatment of Animals and Ingrid Newkirk. Warner Books, 1993.

The Compassionate Gourmet, by Janet Hunt. Thorsons, 1986.

The Cookbook for People Who Love Animals. Gentle World, 1989 (3rd edition).

Cookin' Healthy with One Foot Out the Door: Quick Meals for Fast Times, by Polly Pitchford and Delia Quigley. Book Publishing Company, 1994.

Cooking with Gluten and Seitan, by Dorothy R. Bates and Colby Wingate. Book Publishing Company, 1993.

Country Life Vegetarian Cookbook, from the kitchens of the Country Life Restaurants. Family Health Publications, 1990. Ring bound.

Ecological Cooking: Recipes to Save the Planet, by Joanne Stepaniak and Kathy Hecker. Book Publishing Company, 1992.

Eva Blatt's Vegan Cookery, by Eva Blatt. Thorsons, 1985.

Fabulous Beans, by Barb Bloomfield. Book Publishing Company, 1994.

Food Combining Recipe Book, by Pam Kahn with Dennis Nelson. A 32-page booklet. Natural Hygiene/raw foods. $2 including shipping to C. Olson, P.O. Box 5100, Santa Cruz, CA 95063.

Foods that Cause You to Lose Weight: The Negative Calorie Effect, by Neal Barnard, M.D. Magni, 1995.

Fresh from the Vegetarian Kitchen by Merideth McCarty. St. Martin's Press, 1995.

Friendly Foods: Gourmet Vegetarian Cuisine, by Brother Ron Pickarski, O.F.M., acclaimed vegan caterer to vegetarian and vegan congresses. Ten Speed Press, 1991.

"The Gold Plan," menu plans and nutritional information for institutions. Physicians Committee for Responsible Medicine (see Appendix C: Organizations).

Good Time Eatin' in Cajun Country: Cajun Vegetarian Cuisine by Donna Simón. Book Publishing Company, 1995.

The Gourmet Vegan, by Heather Lamont. Gollancz, 1988.

The High Road to Health: A Vegetarian Cookbook, by Lindsay Wagner and Ariane Spade. Simon & Schuster, 1994. Includes vegetarian arguments and dietary information.

Holiday Diet Book, by Dorothy R. Bates, edited by Neal Barnard, M.D. Magni, 1994.

Instead of Chicken, Instead of Turkey, by Karen Davis. Book Publishing Company, 1993. Conversion of over 100 poultry and egg dishes "in ways that satisfy the taste buds without destroying the birds."

Jewish Vegetarian Cooking, by Rose Freidman. Thorsons, 1992.

The Joy of Not Cooking: Vegetarian Cuisine Cooked Only by the Sun edited by Imar Hutchins, Delights of the Garden Press, P.O. Box 25554, Washington, D.C. Tel: 202-462-5281.

Judy Brown's Guide to Natural Foods Cooking, by Judy Brown. Book Publishing Company, 1989.

The Laurel's Kitchen Bread Book, by Laurel Robertson. Peter Smith Publisher, 1994.

Light Eating for Survival, by Marcia Acciardo. Twenty First Century, 1978. Raw foods.

The Lighthearted Vegetarian Gourmet Cookbook, by Steve Victor. Pacific Press, 1988.

The Lowfat Jewish Vegetarian Cookbook: Healthy Traditions from Around the World, by Debra Wasserman. Vegetarian Resource Group, 1993.

Luscious Low Fat Desserts, by Marie Oser. Chariot Publishing, 1994.

The McDougall Health Supporting Cookbook, by Mary McDougall. Volumes 1 (1985) and 2 (1986).

Meatless Meals for Working People: Quick & Easy Vegetarian Recipes by Debra Wasserman. Vegetarian Resource Group.

Natural Dining: A Cornucopia of Vegetarian Recipes, by Victoria Moran. Trans-Species Unlimited, 1990.

The New Farm Vegetarian Cookbook, edited by Louise Hagler and Dorothy R. Bates. Book Publishing Company, 1988. Almost as fat laden as the original edition in the heady 60s. Good sections on how to make tofu, soy burgers, soy milk, nondairy yogurt cheese, tempeh.

The New Laurel's Kitchen, by Laurel Robertson, Carol Flinders, and Brian Ruppenthal. Ten Speed Press, 1986 (2nd edition). Not vegan.

The New McDougall Cookbook, by John McDougall and Mary McDougall.

No Cholesterol Passover Recipes, by Debra Wasserman. Vegetarian Resource Group, 1995.

The Now and Zen Epicure: Gourmet Cuisine for the Enlightened Palate, by Miyoko Nishimoto. Book Publishing Company, 1991.

Oats, Peas, Beans and Barley Cookbook, by Edith Young Cottrell. Woodbridge Press Publishing Company, 1985.

The Peaceful Palate: Fine Vegetarian Cuisine, by Jennifer Raymond. *The Peaceful Palate* is loosebound and periodically updated.

The Perennial Political Palate: A Feminist Vegetarian Cookbook, Sanguinaria Publishing/Bloodroot Collective, 85 Ferris Street, Bridgeport, CT 06605. Tel: 203-576-9168. Approximately 85% vegan.

Recipes from an Ecological Kitchen, by Lorna J. Sass. William Morrow, 1992. Many recipes quick and easy.

The Sensuous Vegetarian Barbecue, by Vicki Rai Chelf and Cominique Biscoti. Avery, 1994.

The Shoshoni Cookbook: Vegetarian Recipes from the Shoshoni Yoga Spa, by Anne Saks and Faith Stone. Book Publishing Company, 1993.

Simple Food for the Good Life, by Helen Nearing. Stillpoint Publishing, 1985.

Simple, Lowfat & Vegetarian, by Suzanne Havala and Mary Clifford. Vegetarian Resource Group, 1994. 80% nutrition, how to transition, menu makeovers, surviving in restaurants and schools, etc. (vegetarian); 20% recipes (vegan).

Simply Heavenly: The Monastery Vegetarian Cookbook, by Abbot George Burke. Saint George Press, 1995. Vegan.

Simply Vegan: Quick Vegetarian Meals, by Debra Wasserman and Reed Mangels. Vegetarian Resource Group, 1995.

The Single Vegan, by Leah Leneman. Thorsons, 1989.

The Sprout Garden, by Mark Matthew Braunstein. Book Publishing Company, 1993.

Taste and See Allergy Relief Cooking, by Penny King. Family Health Publications, 1992. Religious perspective.

Ten Talents, by Frank J. Hurd and Rosalie Hurd. Ten Talents, 1985. A classic. Vegan except for a short section of transition recipes. Nutritional information, traditional recipes. Ring bound.

Tofu Cookery, by Louise Hagler. Book Publishing Company, 1991.

The TVP Cookbook, by Dorothy R. Bates. Book Publishing Company, 1991. Using texturized vegetable protein.

The Uncheese Cookbook, by Joanne Stepaniak. The Book Publishing Company, 1994.

The Vegan Gourmet, by Susann Geiskopf-Hadler and Mindy Toomay. Prima, 1995.

The Vegan Kitchen, by Freya Dinshah. American Vegan Society, 1988 (11th edition) Ring bound.

Vegetarian Cooking for a Better World, by Muriel C. Golde. Cookbooklet from North American Vegetarian Society.

Vegetarian Cooking for People with Diabetes, by Patricia LeShane. Book Publishing Company, 1994.

Vegetarian Cooking Under Pressure, by Lorna J. Sass. William Morrow, 1994. Includes information on the new generation of pressure cookers.

The Vegetarian No-Cholesterol Cookbook, by Kate Schumann and Virginia Messina. 1995.

Vegetarian Quantity Recipes. Vegetarian Resource Group, 1991. Pack of vegan recipes in serving sizes of 25 and 50, and list of suppliers of vegetarian foods in institutional sizes.

Cookzines

You have to be plugged into the right circles to know what's out there in the home-produced vegan cookzine department, but they're occasionally reviewed in *Vegetarian Journal,* and Vegan Action offers a selection of such 'zines. In general, don't expect cookzines to be necessarily nit-pickingly accurate or reflect medical knowledge about high fat foods. Prices are generally around a couple of bucks. Titles through Vegan Action as of this writing include the following (contact for updated offerings):

Bark & Grass. Great recipes by a real vegan cook—fake meat, more.

Raggedy Anarchy's Guide to Vegan Baking and the Universe. All desserts, all bad for you, all vegan. Lots of rants.

Soy, Not Oi. Humorous, punk rock, drawings, essays, recipes.

Well Fed, Not an Animal Dead. Recipes, organic gardening, breast-feeding, essays.

A couple of other low-cost, home-produced cookbooks are available by sending money to the producers; send a self-addressed stamped postcard for price and to verify if still available:

Seth & Rachel's Vegan Cookbook, by Seth and Rachel. Over 50 recipes on 46 rubber-band-bound pages. Go Vegan, P.O. Box 8, Arrowbear Lake, CA 92382.

The Vegan Revolution Cookbook, by North Woods Vegan Community, Box 953, Ashland, WI 54806. 52 pages, handwritten, mostly vegan.

DataBank

Appendix C: Organizations

Local vegetarian groups are not listed because they are too numerous and in flux, with new ones being formed and old ones disbanding, although some have been around for decades. For an up-to-date list, contact the North American Vegetarian Society, listed below.

American Natural Hygiene Society, 12816 Race Track Road, Tampa, FL 33625. Telephone: 813-855-6607. Natural living and diet, emphasis on raw foods. Publishes *Health Science.*

American Vegan Society, Box H, Malaga, NJ 08328. Telephone: 609-694-2887. Membership includes the quarterly *Ahimsa.* Books and other material by mail.

Canada EarthSave Society, Suite 103, 1093 West Broadway, Vancouver, BC V6H 1E2. Telephone: 604-731-5885.

CoHousing Network, P.O. Box 2584, Berkeley, CA 94702. Telephone: 510-526-6124. Publishes *CoHousing* journal. Not vegetarian. See also Eco-Village listing.

Community Supported Agriculture. Connecting consumers with local organic producers. For a list of CSAs in the U.S. and Canada, call the Bio-dynamic Farming and Gardening Association, 800-516-7797. For the contact person of the CSA nearest you, call Melody Newcombe, editor, *The Harvest Times,* 914-688-5030. CSAs and Biodynamic growing methods are usually not veganic or vegetarian.

Dissection Hotline. Telephone: 800-922-3764 (FROG). Toll-free national help and legal advice line for students forced to dissect. Free handbook "Objecting to Dissection" in three editions: for elementary, high school, and college students. "We are extremely successful at obtaining alternatives for students who have the courage and conviction to see the struggle through to the end."

EarthSave Foundation, 706 Frederick Street, Santa Cruz, CA 95062-2205. Telephone: 408-423-4069; fax: 408-458-0255; orders 800-362-3648. Promoting ecological balance and energy conservation through vegan diet. Local chapters in various cities.

Eco-Village Clearinghouse, 3551 White House Place, Los Angeles, CA 90004. Telephone: 213-738-1254 or 615-964-3992; email: crsp@igc.org. See also CoHousing listing.

Farm Animal Reform Movement (FARM), Box 30654, Bethesda, MD 20824. Telephone: 301-530-1737; fax: 301-530-5747; email: farm@iia.org. Promotes wholesome plant-based diet and improved conditions for farm animals. Organizes annual Great American Meat-Out and other campaigns.

Farm Sanctuary, P.O. Box 150, Watkins Glen, NY 14891. Telephone: 609-583-2225. Vegan organization working with abandoned and rescued animals on the east and west coasts. Farm Sanctuary/West, P.O. Box 1065, Orland, CA 95963. Telephone: 916-865-4617.

Feminists for Animal Rights, P.O. Box 16425, Chapel Hill, NC 27516. Telephone: 919-286-7333. (Editorial: P.O. Box

694, Cathedral Station, New York, NY 10025. Tel: 212-866-6422.) Vegetarian, vegan-oriented, local affiliates in various areas of the country. Publishes newsletter twice a year.

Friends Vegetarian Society of North America (Quaker), P.O. Box 53354, Washington, D.C. 20009. Membership (at press time, $10 regular, $6 low-income) brings quarterly newsletter *The Friendly Vegetarian*.

Fruition, P.O. Box 100, Santa Cruz, CA 95063-0100. Send business-size envelope for information on planting fruit and nut trees in public-access places.

Healthy School Lunch Program, a project of EarthSave, trains people to organize for vegan alternatives in school lunch programs. See appendix A, Further Information.

International Network for Religion and Animals, 2913 Woodstock Avenue, Silver Spring, MD 20910. Telephone: 301-565-9132. Interfaith. Publishes *Inroads* three times a year.

Jewish Vegetarians of North America, 6938 Reliance Road, Federalsburg, MD 21632. For a free sample newsletter, send self-addressed stamped envelope with two first-class stamps.

Kids Against Big Mac, P.O. Box 287, London NW6, U.K. Encourages the formation of local KABM groups around the world to counter the propaganda McDonalds aims at children. Send international reply coupon (available at post office) with inquiry.

McLibel Support Campaign Press Office/U.S., P.O. Box 62, Craftsbury, VT 05826-0062. Telephone/fax: 802-586-9628; email: dbriars@world.std.com. In England: McLibel Support Campaign, c/o 5 Caledonian Road, London N1 9DX, United Kingdom. Telephone/fax: +44-171-713-1269. Organizing support for the vegans in London charged with libel by McDonalds.

North American Vegetarian Society, P.O. Box 72, Dolgeville, NY 13329. Telephone: 518-568-7970. Membership includes the quarterly journal *Vegetarian Voice*. Information on vegetarianism and veganism, a brochure on answers to the most commonly asked questions. Projects include promoting World Vegetarian Day (October 1) and Vegetarian Awareness Month (October); the Vegetarian Fast Food Campaign, to get fast-food chains to serve vegetarian or vegan items; and an annual Summerfest. Books by mail.

People for the Ethical Treatment of Animals (PETA), P.O. Box 42516, Washington, D.C. 20015. Telephone: 301-770-7382 (PETA); fax: 301-770-7324.

Physicians Committee for Responsible Medicine (PCRM), P.O. Box 6322, Washington, D.C. 20015. Telephone: 202-686-2210. Information on diet, nutrition, and health. Publishes *Good Medicine*, "The Right Bite" nutritional curriculum for teachers, and pamphlets on diabetes, heart disease, AIDS, weight control, and other health issues.

Toronto Vegetarian Association, 736 Bathurst Street, Toronto ON M5S 2R4, Canada. Telephone: 416-533-3897; email: tva@interlog.com. Largest *local* vegetarian society in North America, with 1,400 members.

United Farm Workers, P.O. Box 62, Keene, CA 93531. Telephone: 805-822-5571. Conducting a boycott of table grapes to get growers to stop using the most deadly agricultural chemicals. Written materials, free videotapes in English and Spanish.

Vegan Action, P.O. Box 4353, Berkeley, CA 94704. Telephone: 510-654-6297; email: leor@mellers1.psych.berkeley.edu; World Wide Web: http://envirolink.org/arrs/va/vegan_action.html. Information on vegan diets and how to promote veganism.

Vegan CoHousing Organizing Group, P.O. Box 40684, San Francisco, CA 94140. Send SASE for newsletter, including email address, if you have one. Recommended reading: *CoHousing: A Contemporary Approach to Housing Ourselves* by Kathryn McCamsant and Charles Durrett, with Ellen Hertzman.

Vegans International, c/o Cor Nouws, coordinator, Postbus 1087, 6801 Arnhem BB, The Netherlands. Telephone: +31 (0)85 420746. U.S. country coordinator: Chas Chiodo, Route 4, Box 585, Alachua, FL 32615. Telephone: 904-462-5309. Newsletter. U.S. email: maxout@uclink2.berkeley.edu.

The Vegan Society, 7 Battle Road, St. Leonards-on-Sea, E. Sussex TH27 7AA, United Kingdom. Telephone: 44-424-427393. For email address, check Vegan-L mailing list, Appendix H: Vegetarian Online Resources.

Vegan Society of Australia, Box 85, Seaford, VIC 3198, Telephone: (03) 862-1686. Also vegan societies in NSW and South Brisbane, and vegan-sympathetic groups elsewhere.

Vegan World, P.O. Box 2565, Marco Island, FL 33969. Telephone: 813-642-1000. Promotes vegetarianism and veganism.

Vegetarian Awareness Network, P.O. Box 321, Knoxville, TN 37901. Telephone: 800-548-8343 (KIT-VEGE). For free vegetarian information packet, send name, address, phone number, and four first-class stamps. Also sells books and tapes, and refers callers to their nearest vegetarian society. Volunteer staffed.

Vegetarian Information Network & Exchange (VINE), P.O. Box 2224, Ann Arbor, MI 48106. Telephone: 313-668-9925; email: vine-info@umich.edu. Focuses on info by email.

Vegetarian Nutrition Center, Wolfson Campus, Miami-Dade Community College, 300 NE 2nd Avenue, Miami, FL 33132. Telephone: 305-237-7632. Cooking classes (English and Spanish), plus nutrition, yoga, bodywork, and sports nutrition.

Vegetarian Nutrition Dietetic Practice Group, American Dietetic Association, 216 W. Jackson Blvd., Chicago, IL 60606. Telephone: 312-899-0040, extension 4602. For nutritional info or referral to the Area Coordinator of the VNDPG for your area, call toll-free 800-366-1655 (bilingual English/Spanish).

Vegetarian Resource Center, P.O. Box 38-1068, Cambridge, MA 02238-1068. Telephone: 617-625-3790; email: vrc@tiac.net. Supports formation of local vegetarian groups, especially in the northeast.

Vegetarian Resource Group, P.O. Box 1463, Baltimore, MD 21203. Telephone: 410-366-VEGE (-8343); email: TheVRG@ aol.com Promotes vegetarian and vegan diet, provides nutritional information (including a flyer in Spanish), and publishes books and the quarterly *Vegetarian Journal*, free of advertising. Food projects for children, ethical career choice for high school and college students, how to start a vegetarian group at your school, nutrition for teens, vegetarian videos for loan, veganism and pregnancy, lactation, childhood, and vegan recipes for institutional use.

Vegetarians International Voice for Animals (Viva!), P.O. Box 212, Crewe, CW1 4SD, UK. Telephone: +44-1270-522500; fax: 522511. Send international reply coupon (available at post office) and/or donation for the *Convert-A-Parent* booklet (see Appendix A: Further Information).

Vegetarian Society of the United Kingdom (VSUK), Parkdale, Dunham Road, Altrincham, Cheshire, WA14 4QG, England. Telephone: (0161) 928-0793; fax: 0161-926-9182; email: vegsoc@vegsoc.demon.co.uk (begin message with "Hi Veg Soc"). World Wide Web: http://catless.ncl.ac.uk/Vegetarian/Veg Soc UK/info.html. Publishes *The Vegetarian* magazine, four issues/year.

Vegetarian Union of North America, P.O. Box 9710, Washington, D.C. 20016. Telephone: 617-625-3790; email: vrc@tiac.net. USA affiliate of International Vegetarian Union (IVU), 10 Kings Drive, Marple, Stockport, Cheshire, SK6 6NQ, England. Works with vegetarian groups and helps organize conferences.

Youth for Environmental Sanity (YES!), 706 Frederick Street, Santa Cruz, CA 95062-2205. Telephone: 408-459-9344. National tours of groups of young people speaking to junior and senior high school assemblies about the environment and what youth can do to save it, including vegetarian and vegan food choices. Affiliated with EarthSave.

Alternatives to Allopathic Medicine

Allopathic medicine—what most of us think of when we talk of medicine—is great for things like setting broken bones and emergency, life-saving surgery, but there are other medical modalities that are increasingly popular. Allopaths usually lump them together as "alternative" medicine. See also Appendix A: Further Information, for books on alternative medicine.

American Association of Acupuncture and Oriental Medicine, 1424 16th Street N.W., #501, Washington, D.C. 20036. Telephone: 202-265-2287.

American Association of Naturopathic Physicians, 2800 East Madison, Suite 200, Seattle, WA 98113. Telephone: 206-323-7610, recording only. For brochure and national listing of member physicians, send $5 to AANP, 2366 Eastlake Avenue East, Suite 322, Seattle, WA 98102, or fax with credit card number and expiration to 206-323-7612.

American Botanical Council, P.O. Box 201660, Austin, TX 78720. Telephone: 512-331-8868.

American Chiropractic Association, 1701 Clarendon Boulevard, Arlington, VA 22209. Telephone: 703-276-8800.

American Holistic Medical Association, 4101 Lake Boone Trail, Suite 201, Raleigh, NC 27607. Telephone: 919-787-5146. ($5 for list of members.)

National Center for Homeopathy, 801 N. Fairfax St., Fairfax, VA 22314. Telephone: 703-548-7790.

Hunger and Development Organizations

The Whole Foods Project is organized by the Tides Foundation, 115 E. 23rd Street, 10th Floor, New York, NY 10010. Telephone: 212-420-1828. Food and other services provided out of Rutgers Presbyterian Church, 236 W. 73rd Street. Organic vegan meals to people with AIDS, HIV, cancer, and heart disease in New York City; cooking classes and nutrition information; and support groups. Available to help other groups start up or shift toward organic vegan foods. Committed to serving as many meals as needed, and then working to find funding; all donations, large and small, welcome.

Food Not Bombs is a network of independent groups in dozens of U.S. cities that feed vegetarian, often vegan and organic, food to the homeless in highly visible places while making the connection between high military spending, cutbacks in social support services, and increasing social problems. Chapters in Europe and Israel, and perhaps in other parts of the world by the time you read this. Donations of money, food, or time welcomed, and they can help you start a local group in your area. Western U.S.: FNB, 3145 Geary Boulevard. No. 12, San Francisco, CA 94118. Telephone: 800-884-1136. Eastern U.S.: FNB, 295 Forest Ave. No. 314, Portland, ME 04101. Telephone: 800-569-4054. Outside the U.S.: contact either address.

"Plenty" helps poor people in other countries and Native Americans here develop self-sufficiency, including growing soybeans and building soy dairies, developing fair trade relationships, protecting the environment and human rights, and developing radio communications. Sponsors a "Kids to the Country" skills and recreation camp for inner-city American youth. Publishes *A Guide to Growing and Using Soybeans for Food* and the cookbook *Recipes from the Global Kitchen*. Donations, orders, and inquiries welcome to Plenty, P.O. Box 394, Summertown, TN 38483. Telephone/fax: 615-964-4864.

Vegfam "feeds the hungry [abroad] without exploiting animals." Provides short-term and long-term food aid and funds projects like irrigation, conservation, and tree planting, in agriculturally depressed areas. Donations to Vegfam: The Sanctuary, Nr. Lydford, Devon, EX20 4AL,

U.K. Telephone: (0)822-82203 or (0)462-56294. Registered British Charity No. 232208. Write (with two International Postal Reply Coupons, available from the Post Office) or call to verify current address and find out the best way to make a donation from outside the U.K.

Contact your local **Seventh Day Adventists church.** If you can't locate one, call 301-680-6733 for the one nearest you.

Hare Krishna groups distribute free vegetarian food in some cities. Look in the phone book under "Hare Krishna" or "International Society for Krishna Consciousness."

Sex, Romance, and Friendship

Being vegetarian or vegan can be a lonely experience, especially if you find yourself not wanting to "kiss lips that touch meat" (or milk). If you're cut off from others of your ilk, there are matchmaking services that cater to you. Even if sexual or romantic sparks don't fly, such a service can result in good friendships.

The following services advertise, but have not been checked; that's your responsibility—take it seriously. They are *not* necessarily a vegetarian service, but are likely to have a higher than usual percentage of vegetarians. A person who registers as vegetarian or vegan may be describing either a general dietary tendency or a commitment; ask specific questions.

Before joining a service, find out if it fits you. Ask their prices, how long they've been in existence, the number of new registrants in a typical month, other values they may assume or promote (e.g., ecology, particular political or religious values, etc.), whether they have categories for vegetarian or vegan, how clearly they define the terms for registrants—and if they offer any money-back guarantees. If you're looking for someone who is monogamous or polyamorous, gay, bi, lesbian, hetero, vegan, Jewish, vege-tarian, atheist, born-again Christian, recovering Catholic, or whatever, ask what percent of their registrants are so, in general and in your area. If a service is not willing or able to be explicit about who and what it does and does not cater to, go with another service.

At the Gate, Box 09506, Columbus, OH 43209. "Vegetarian singles concerned with animal rights, ecology, spirituality, personal growth." Free info.

Concerned Singles, Box 555, Stockbridge, MA 01262. Not specifically for vegetarians, but for "compatible singles who care about the environment, personal growth, and peace." All ages. Free sample of newsletter on request.

CSC, 212-873-7187. "Helps growth/health-oriented singles meet through events, newsletter. Now national. Call anytime."

Left Coast Vegetarian Singles, 1875 South Bascom Avenue, Suite 116-278, Campbell, CA 95008. For vegetari-ans on the left (= west) coast.

Natural Match, 131 Bloor Street West, Suite 200-275, Toronto, Ontario M5S 1R8, Canada.

Singles, Box 310, Allardt, TN 38504. For "nice singles with Christian values. Nationwide. Free magazine. Send age, interests."

Vegetarian International Pen Club (VIP), P.O. Box 2036, Tempe, AZ 85280. Telephone: 602-352-4383; email: ocatilla@-garden.com. Sample copy $3. A number of listings are apparently not vegetarian, but cross-listings from general international pen pal clubs and magazines.

Vegetarian Singles News, a monthly magazine. Subscription includes free personal ad. Expensive 900 number to call to leave messages for people with listings. Two weekly calls free to an 800 number to pick up mes-sages. Info: 800-WIN-VEGI (946-8344).

DataBank

Appendix D:
Cruelty-Free Products

Not all products from the following companies may be vegan or vegetarian. Ask when you contact them.

Feeding Companion Animals

Famous Fido's Doggie Deli Inc., 1533 W. Devon Avenue, Chicago, IL 60660. Telephone: 312-761-6028. Vegetarian foods and treats for dogs.

Harbingers for a New Age, 717 E. Missoula Avenue, Troy, MT 59935-9609. Telephone: 406-295-4944 (orders: 800-884-6262). Manufacturers of Vegepet supplements and publishers of the book *Vegetarian Cats and Dogs* by James Peden. Vegan.

Natural Life Pet Products, Inc., Frontenac, Kansas 66762. Telephone: 800-367-2391. Dog food.

Nature's Recipe, 341 Bonnie Circle, Corona, CA 91720. Telephone: 800-843-4008. Vegan canned and dry dog food.

Pet Guard, P.O. Box 728, Orange Park, FL 32067-0728. Telephone: 800-874-3221. Vegan canned dog food.

Wow-Bow Distributors, 309 Burr Road, East Northport, NY 11731. Telephone: 516-449-8572, 800-326-0230, or 800-843-4008.

Wysong Corporation, Dept. CF, 1880 N. Eastman Avenue, Midland, MI 48640. Telephone: 800-748-0188. Vegetarian cat food.

Cruelty-Free Personal and Household Products

Most personal care and household cleaning substances have been force-fed to animals, patched on their shaved skin, or squirted into their eyes to see just how toxic they are. Products free of such cruelty are gaining popularity, but unfortunately the term "cruelty-free" has no legal definition, and is sometimes abused. There are several things to remember.

So many companies—both mainstream and "natural"—test on animals or use animal products that it's safe to assume that a given product or company involves animal cruelty unless you know otherwise. A cruelty-free company should be willing to tell you, on the label or in a letter to you.

Even well-meaning people misuse the term "cruelty-free" to mean only that the product was not tested on animals. It may still have animal by-products as ingredients, and therefore not be really cruelty free. Ask specifically about testing and ingredients including animal "by-products."

Some manufacturers of cruelty-free products buy their bulk ingredients from suppliers who have tested them on animals. Ask for a written statement that suppliers do not test on animals or contract out for testing to be done.

Some companies used to test on animals or bought from suppliers who did, but have now adopted a strict policy against it. Reward them for their change of heart. A few compassionate and far-sighted companies have had such a policy for many years. Reward them with your preferential buying.

Testing Toys on Animals

Some toy companies used to test their products on animals. Chemicals would be tested for toxicity by putting them on an animal's skin, or in her eye, or force-feeding it to her. Projectile toys might be tested on animals to see if they would break the skin or put out an eye. Because a lot of people stopped buying toys from those companies—and let them know why with letters—they stopped.

Cruelty-Free Drums

Animal products can be found in many things. For example, if you like to pound on African drums or thump on Middle Eastern ones, you know that the heads are usually made with animal skins. But there are Middle Eastern metal or ceramic doumbeks available with synthetic heads, available at or through music stores, and from Moshe Halfon, 57 Westchester Drive, Attleboro, MA 02703.

A traditional African variable-tone "talking drum" is made with a vegan head by Laughing Crow Arts, 25370 Wolf Creek Road, Crow, OR 94787. Telephone: 503-935-3372. The owners are also opening a vegan bed and breakfast and retreat on the Oregon coast: "Traditionally these drums were made of wood and goat hide. [We] decided to create a talking drum using alternative, gentle materials. The result is a professional-caliber instrument made of high-fire stoneware and Fiberskyn."

High-quality synthetic drum heads cost about twice as much as animal-skin heads, but are superior because they're impervious to changes in temperature and humidity. The cost of the head is not the main cost of a drum. You can buy a conga drum body, or a second-hand drum with a busted head, and have the drum head replaced with a synthetic head (Fiberskyn 2 is reportedly superior to the original Fiberskyn). Where there's a will, there's a way.

DataBank

Appendix E: Mail Order Food and Sustainable Agriculture

Mail Order Food

For those not fortunate enough to live near a good natural food store or co-op, or who wish to save money by ordering in bulk, many natural, organic, and/or transitional vegan/vegetarian foods are available by mail. Write or call for free catalogs and price lists. Look in natural foods publications for additional or new mail order businesses.

Arrowhead Mills, P.O. Box 2059, Hereford, TX 79045. Telephone: 800-858-4308. Organic flours, grains, beans, seeds, oils, peanut butter, and tahini (sesame "butter").

Frankferd Farms, 717 Saxonburg Boulevard, Saxonburg, PA 16056. Telephone: 412-898-2242. Organic flour, grains, and macrobiotic foods.

Gold Mine Natural Food Company, 1947 30th Street, San Diego, CA 92102-1105. Telephone: 800-475-3663. Macrobiotic. Misos, oils, nuts, seeds, beans, and non caffeine "coffees."

Harvest Direct, P.O. Box 4514, Decatur, IL 62525. Telephone: 800-835-2867. Texturized vegetable protein, herbs, etc.

Herb and Spice Collection, Frontier Cooperative Herb, P.O. Box 299, Norway, IA 52318. Telephone: 800-786-1388. Nonirradiated herbs, spices, extracts, and herbal seasonings, vegan bacon bits, oils, etc. (Note: supermarket herbs are usually irradiated.)

Jaffe Brothers, P.O. Box 636, Valley Center, CA 92082. Telephone: 619-749-1133. Organic dried fruits, nuts, seeds, grains, oils, etc.

Lumen, P.O. Box 350, Lake Charles, LA 70602-0350. Telephone: 318-436-6748. Natural ingredient vegan "meats."

Rainbow Natural Foods, 1487 Richmond Road, Ottawa, Ontario K2B 6R9, Canada. Telephone: 613-726-9200.

Shiloh, P.O. Box 97, Sulphur Springs, AR 72768-0097. Telephone: 800-362-6832.

Soyfoods Center, P.O. Box 234, Lafayette, CA 94549. Telephone: 415-283-2991. Catalog.

The Date People, P.O. Box 2328, Borrego Springs, CA 92004. Telephone: 619-540-5693. Wide variety of organic dates.

The Mail Order Catalog, Box 180, Summertown, TN 38483. Telephone: 800-695-2241. Books, vegan and vegetarian cookbooks, nutritional yeast flakes (the good-tasting kind), starter for making tempeh, instant gluten flour.

The Mountain Ark Trader, 120 South East Avenue, Fayetteville, AR 72702. Telephone: 800-643-8909. Macrobiotic cooking equipment and foods, including agar (vegan sea-vegetable "gelatin") and toasted sesame oil.

Vermont Country Maple, Inc., P.O. Box 53, Jericho Center, VT 05465. Telephone: 802-864-7519. Maple syrup and granulated maple sugar.

Walnut Acres, Penns Creek, PA 17862. Telephone: 800-433-3998. Organic produce, fruits, flours, grain, "one of the finest peanut butters available," hickory-smoked nutritional yeast, kitchenware.

Sustainable Farming and Gardening

Veganic

Resources for those wishing to farm or garden without the use of slaughterhouse and factory farm products such as blood and bone meal and animal manure. Research is being done on "stockless rotations" at several U.S. universities. There are varying degrees of veganicness in veganic farming, with the most veganic involving looking for ways to deal with pests with the minimum of killing. The baseline, though, is avoidance of fertilizers that require exploitation of animals and sea creatures.

Elm Farm Research Centre, Hamstead Marshall, Nr Newbury, Berks RG15 OHR, United Kingdom. Ongoing research since 1987 into veganic farming, both onsite and by compiling data from veganic farms in Germany, Austria, and elsewhere.

Khadigar, Box 1167, Farmington, ME 04938, is currently the only veganic farm in the USA. (There are, of course, a number of veganic gardens, some of which may be production gardens for farmers markets, and probably a good number of de facto veganic or near-organic farms using "green manures".)

Veganic Gardening: The Alternative System for Healthier Crops. A book by Kenneth Dalziel O'Brien. Available from American Vegan Society.

Organic

ATTRA News, quarterly newsletter of Appropriate Technology Transfer to Rural Areas, National Center for Appropriate Technology, P.O. Box 3657, Fayetteville, AR 72702. Telephone: 800-346-9140.

Alternative Farming Systems Information Center, National Agriculture Library, 10301 Baltimore Boulevard, Beltsville, MD 20705-2351. Telephone: 301-504-6927; email: nalafsic@nalusda.gov. Literature includes "Educational and

Training Opportunities in Sustainable Agriculture" and an extensive bibliography of "Green Manures and Cover Crops." For farmers, not individual consumers.

Biodynamic Farming and Gardening Association. Telephone: 800-516-7797. Referrals to Community Supported Agriculture network in your area.

California Certified Organic Farmers, 1115 Mission Street, Santa Cruz, CA 95060. Telephone: 408-423-2263; email: ccof@igc.apc.org.

Healthy Harvest III: A Directory of Sustainable Agriculture and Horticulture Organizations. From agAccess, Davis, CA. Telephone: 916-756-7177.

National Organic Program, TMD/AMS/USDA, P.O. Box 96456, Room 2510-South, Washington, D.C. 20090-6456. Telephone: 202-720-3252. The agency in charge of overseeing the new national organic standards and of any "amendments" to the authorizing legislation (e.g., instituting "veganic" labeling for organic crops grown with only "green manures" or "stockless rotations").

If you want to find a job working on an organic farm or locate organic farmers near where you live, ask around at your local farmers market or natural food store, or contact the organic certifying agency. Because the term "veganic" is not generally known in organic gardening circles, if inquiring about veganic methods, you may need to ask around for farmers who use "green manures" and "stockless rotations."

DataBank

Appendix F:
Vegetarian Celebrities

The following is adapted from a list in the February 1994 issue of *Vegetarian Times*. A number of these persons are vegan, but the listing doesn't distinguish between vegan and vegetarian. These are confirmed vegetarian celebrities, and one may assume that there are many more vegetarian celebrities who were not queried for this list, and so were excluded.

Henry (Hank) Aaron, major league baseball home run champion

Ridgely Abele, world champion in karate

Bryan Adams, rock musician

Carol Adams, feminist author

Stephen Admonson, rock bassist in Paradise Lost

Grant Aleksander, star of TV's *Guiding Light*.

Jon Anderson, rock vocalist in Yes

Maxine Andrews, singer in the Andrews Sisters

Piers Anthony, author

Matt Archer, rock drummer in Paradise Lost

Joan Armatrading, rock vocalist

Rosanna Arquette, actress

Marty Balin, rock musician, founding member of Jefferson Starship

Bob Barker, TV personality

Peter Barnes, founder of Working Assets (recently renamed Citizens Trust)

Rachel Barton, classical violinist

Kim Basinger, actress

Meredith Baxter, actress

Elizabeth (Betsy) Beard, member of 1988 U.S. Olympic rowing team

Jeff Beck, rock guitarist

Ed Begley Jr., actor

Dirk Benedict, author, actor

Rose Bird, Chief Justice of California Supreme Court, 1977–1986

Herbert Blomstedt, conductor of the San Francisco Symphony Orchestra

Cindy Blum, opera singer

Surya Bonalyl, Olympic medalist in ice skating

David Bowie, rock musician

Boy George, rock vocalist

Berke Breathed, cartoonist

Christie Brinkley, model and actress

Brigid Brophy, author

Roger Brown, professional football player

Faina Bryanskaya, classical pianist

Ellen Burstyn, actress

Peter Burwash, Davis Cup winner, tennis professional

Kate Bush, rock vocalist

Joy Bush, powerlifting champion

Bernard Butler, rock guitarist in Suede

Andreas Cahling, champion bodybuilder, Mr. International

Andrew Calhoun, musician

Kirk Cameron, actor

Chris Campbell, Olympic bronze medalist in wrestling

Benjamin Carson, M.D., prominent neurosurgeon

Andrei Codrescu, poet and radio personality

Sue Coe, artist

Phil Collen, rock guitarist in Def Leppard

Peter Cox, author

Jack Dangers, rock musician in Meat Beat Manifesto

Gary Daniels, actor and karate expert

Dave Davies, rock musician in the Kinks

Ray Davies, rock musician in the Kinks

Patti Davis, author

Skeeter Davis, country singer

Alexandra Day (Sandra Darling), children's illustrator/author

James de Donato, world record swimmer

Jonathan de Donato, world record swimmer

Anthony John Dennison, actor

Harvey and Marilyn Diamond, cookbook authors

Lee Dorrian, rock singer in Cathedral

Joe Elliott, guitarist in Def Leppard

Elvira, actress and TV personality

Melissa Etheridge, rock singer

Peter Falk, actor

Gary Fanelli, marathon winner

Tim Finn, rock musician

Michael W. Fox, author

Michael Franks, jazz singer

Peter Gabriel, rock musician

Ina Mae Gaskin, midwifery activist

Steven Gaskin, author and founder of The Farm

Sara Gilbert, actress

Philip Glass, composer

David and Nikki Goldbeck, authors

Bobcat Goldthwaite, comedian and actor

Lecy Goranson, actress

Elliot Gould, actor

Estelle Gray and Cheryl Marek, world record cross-country tandem cyclists

Dick Gregory, comedian and activist

Scott Hackwith, rock vocalist in Dig

Nina Hagen, rock vocalist

Holly Hallstrom, TV personality

Cecelia Hammond, model

Richie Havens, folk-rock musician

Kane Hodder, stuntman

Ruth Heidrich, Ironman triathlete, age-group record holder

Henry Heimlich, M.D., physician, inventor of the Heimlich maneuver

Doug Henning, magician

Roy Hilligan, bodybuilder

Dustin Hoffman, actor

Nick Holmes, rock singer in Paradise Lost

Hans Holzer, author

Desmond Howard, Heisman trophy winner

Steve Howe, guitarist in Yes
Laura Huxley, author
Chrissie Hynde, rock musician in the Pretenders
Michael Jackson, rock musician
Andrew Jacobs Jr., member of Congress from Indiana
Gaz Jennings, rock guitarist in Cathedral
Steve Jobs, computer whiz
Eric Johnson, rock guitarist
Kathy Johnson, Olympic silver medalist in gymnastics
Jill Johnston, author
Davy Jones, musician and actor
Howard Jones, rock musician
China Kantner, actress and deejay
Romy Karz, ballerina
Casey Kasem, radio and TV personality
Mollie Katzen, cookbook author and artist
Jim Kerr, rock musician
Anthony Kiedes, singer in the Red Hot Chili Peppers
Kay Kimler, stuntwoman and stunt coordinator
Billie Jean King, tennis champion
Michael Klaper, M.D., author and nutrition advocate
Barbara Ann Klein, stuntwoman
Killer Kowalski, champion wrestler
KRS-ONE, rap musician
k.d. lang, country-rock singer
R.D. Laing, physician and author
Tony La Russa, manager of the Oakland A's
Frances Moore Lappé, author and world-hunger activist
Maria Lauren, actress
Sabina Le Beauf, actress

Cloris Leachman, actress
Adam Lehan, rock guitarist in Cathedral
Jarrett Lennon, actor
Annie Lennox, rock vocalist
Phil Lesh, musician in the Grateful Dead
Marv Levy, head coach of the Buffalo Bills
Carl Lewis, Olympic runner
Tom Leykus, radio personality
Sixto Linares, triathlete
Peggy Lipton, actress
Isabel Lorca, actress
Lene Lovich, rock vocalist
Harold Lyman, lecturer
Dana Lyons, children's musician
John McDougall, M.D., author, radio and TV show host
Gregor Mackintosh, rock guitarist in Paradise Lost
Patrick Macnee, actor
Catherine Malfitano, opera singer
Bill Manetti, powerlifting champion
Steve Martin, comedian and actor
Jim Mason, author
Paul and Linda McCartney, rock musicians
Colman McCarthy, syndicated columnist
Michael Medved, author and film critic
Natalie Merchant, rock vocalist
Dan Millman, world champion gymnast
Donna Mills, actress
Hayley Mills, actress
Michael Mish, children's musician
Matthew Modine, actor

Karen Moran, author and psychologist

Victoria Moran, author

Morrissey, rock vocalist

Edwin Moses, Olympic gold medalist in track

Johnette Napolitano, rock vocalist in Concrete Blonde

Martina Navrotilova, tennis champion

Kevin Nealon, comedian

Helen Nearing, author, pioneer of back-to-the-land movement

Olivia Newton-John, rock vocalist

Stevie Nicks, rock musician in Fleetwood Mac

Gary Null, author

Paavo Nurmi, long-distance runner with twenty world records

Laura Nyro, rock vocalist and pianist

Al Oerter, discus thrower and winner of four Olympic gold medals

Ogre, rock musician in Skinny Puppy

Meghan O'Leary, bodybuilder

Gayle Olinekova, triathlete

Dean Ornish, M.D., cardiologist and author

Ken Owen, rock drummer in Carcass

Bill Pearl, four-time Mr. Universe, bodybuilder, and author

Leander Paes, Junior Wimbledon champion

Jizzy Pearl, rock vocalist in Love/Hate

Diane Pfiefer, author

Bill Pickering, swam the English Channel

Kate Pierson, rock vocalist in the B-52s

Martha Plimpton, actress

Tracy Pollan, actress

Stan Price, world record holder in bench press

Linnea Quigley, actress

Raffi, children's musician

Sherry Ramsey, star of TV's *Guiding Light*

Phylicia Rashad, actress

Amy Ray, rock vocalist in the Indigo Girls

Tom Regan, author and teacher

Ruth Rendell, author

Jeremy Rifkin, author and activist

Julie Ritter, rock vocalist in Mary's Danish

Anthony Robbins, author and motivational speaker

John Robbins, author and environmental activist

Bobby Rock, drummer in Nelson

Fred Rogers, TV's "Mister Rogers"

Murray Rose, world record swimmer

Howard Rosenberg, syndicated columnist

Ric Rubin, record producer, founder of American Records

Todd Rundgren, rock musician

William Sadler, actor

John Salley, basketball player with Miami Heat

Boz Scaggs, rock musician

Michael Schenker, rock guitarist

Fred Schneider, rock vocalist in the B-52s

Tom Scholtz, rock musician

Dave Scott, six-time Ironman triathlon winner

Michael Sembello, pop singer/songwriter

Shankar and Caroline, world musicians

Corky Siegel, blues musician

Peter Singer, philosopher, author, and animal rights advocate

Grace Slick, founding member of Jefferson Airplane

Anthony Smedile, rock drummer in Dig

Kelly Shaye Smith, actress

Shawn Smity, junior kayaking champion

Debbie Spaeth-Herring, Georgia State champion powerlifter

Sy Sperling, president of the Hair Club for Men

Rick Springfield, rock musician

Bill Steer, rock guitarist in Carcass

Johnny Stephens, rock musician in Meat Beat Manifesto

Michael Stipe, musician in R.E.M.

Larry Storch, actor

Robert Sweetgall, long-distance walker

Leigh Taylor-Young, actress

Robert Tepper, singer/songwriter

John Tesh, TV personality

Cicely Tyson, actress

Steve Vai, rock guitarist

Eddie Vedder, rock vocalist in Pearl Jam

Lindsay Wagner, actress

Jeff Walker, rock vocalist in Carcass

Dave Wallechinsky, author

Robert James Waller, author

Lesley Ann Warren, actress

Rosalind Warren, author

Dennis Weaver, actor and activist

Tico Wells, actor

Tim Wheater, flutist

Forrest Whitaker, actor

Ann Wigmore, author and wheat grass authority
Spice Williams, actress, stuntwoman, and bodybuilder
Wendy O. Williams, rock vocalist
Vanessa Williams, actress
Gretchen Wyler, actress
Ahmet Zappa, rock vocalist

A Few Famous Vegetarians Throughout History

Bronson Alcott
Louisa May Alcott
Clara Barton
Annie Besant
Cesar Chavez
Leonardo da Vinci
Charles Darwin
Isadora Duncan
Thomas Edison
Albert Einstein
Mahatma Gandhi
Sylvester Graham
Horace Greeley
John Harvey Kellogg
John Milton
Malcolm Muggeridge
Scott Nearing
Sir Isaac Newton
Ovid
Plato

Plutarch
Alexander Pope
Porphyry
Pythagoras
Jean Jacques Rousseau
Henry Salt
Satchidananda
Albert Schweitzer
Seneca
George Bernard Shaw
Mary Wollstonecraft Shelley
Percy Bysshe Shelley
Upton Sinclair
Isaac Bashevis Singer
Socrates
Leo Tolstoy
Peter Tosh
Voltaire
H.G. Wells
Ellen G. White
Esmé Wynne-Tyson

DataBank

Appendix G:
Getting Vegan Food in
Institutions/Vegetarian Elders

The current revitalization and veganization of the vegetarian movement is coming primarily from the kids, teens, and college students, who are challenging the dietary ways of the institutions they participate in, from schools right down to the family. Vegan Action, based in Berkeley, California, is promoting student campaigns to get full vegan meals in college and university cafeterias, while Santa Cruz, California based EarthSave has produced a manual for those who want to get a vegan alternative food line in primary and secondary school systems.

For information on how to get vegan meals into elementary and secondary schools, refer to the *Healthy School Lunch Action Guide,* from EarthSave. (See Appendix C: Organizations.)

Colleges and Universities—How to Start a Vegan Dorm Food Campaign*

In the fall of 1994, students at the University of California at Berkeley saw a deficiency in the dining options in the residence halls. While the dining halls served vegetarian entrees, there was no vegan option. In response to this, Students in Support of Animals waged a campaign to implement a vegan entree at every meal. After four months of campaigning, the student group was successful in making UC Berkeley the largest major public university to offer a vegan entree at every meal. The following is a modification of their game plan.

General Campaign Strategies

For a successful campaign, certain strategies should be used. The most important factor in waging an effective campaign is to mainstream the idea of a vegan dorm option. This was done at Berkeley by appealing to health and environmental groups as well. Framing the idea of a vegan dorm option in those terms appeals to a wider range of students and will get more student groups involved in the effort. It is very important not to treat the vegan option as a purely animal rights issue. This would only alienate people not associated with the animal rights movement.

For example, instead of saying "We are advocating a vegan diet," it may be more effective to say, "We are advocating a more healthy, environmentally sound, plant-based diet."

It is also very important to work with the university whenever possible. University administrators are more likely to change if their initial impression of the student

*Reprinted with permission of Vegan Action

group is positive. For this reason, we do not suggest starting your campaign with a demonstration or protest. First, try the nice-guy approach. Chances are that, if you are well-organized, it will work. If meetings, petitions, and letter writing don't produce significant results, then consider other tactics.

In general the things to keep in mind are:

- This is a positive campaign.
- The issues involved are those of choice.
- The campaign works to increase options rather than limit them.
- Since there are many environmental and heath conscious students, and since many people might want different dorm standards, this campaign is sure to bring a large constituency.

Getting Started

Before starting this campaign, find out who you are going to be working with. For example:

- Is there anyone in student government who is sympathetic to the cause? These people are crucial in setting up meetings with administrators and possibly bringing legislative support. You should seek them out. For example, through our governmental "contact" we got the student senate at Berkeley to unanimously support a bill calling for vegan options.
- Are there any health or environmental organizations that might want to help. The university and students are more likely to respect a joint effort.
- Is there any group that focuses on student rights? Everyone should have the right to eat a nice vegan

meal! Contact any of these groups and find out whether they would be willing to work on this campaign.

- Once you know which groups will be interesting in helping, find out what university officials you will be working with. Who is the person responsible for making decisions in terms of dining hall policies? Are there any university officials (faculty/staff) who will endorse your plan?

Find out from students what the dormitory policies are and what students like/dislike about the dorms. For example, we found that many people were concerned with the problem of inaccurate or deficient labeling of ingredients in dishes. Also, people didn't want high-fat foods. However, many students did like the frozen yogurt soft serve machine. Thus, our campaign called for better labeling, but did not call for the "abolition" of frozen yogurt.

Also, it is highly beneficial to have a press contact (either in a local, or student paper). Our campaign was written about before we ever met with any officials and the article therefore gave an incentive for administrators to act.

Petitioning and Letter Writing

The best way to express student will is through having people sign a petition and write letters. Write a petition that is *positive* (calls for more options rather than a limitation), *inclusive of environmental/health issues, responsive to student needs,* and *short and simple* (in other words, concise!).

Here's the petition we used:

We, the undersigned residents of the University of California dormitories and patrons of Cal Dining

*Services, request that at least one healthy entree with-
out meat, dairy, eggs, or other animal products
(vegan) be served at each meal. We also request that
all food be properly labeled showing all ingredients so
that diners may be assured that the food being served
meets their dietary specifications.*

Give the petition to dorm residents who will have
their friends sign it. Also, it is wise to petition people as
they walk into the dorms. Set up petition tables outside
the dining halls. Remember, *keep it positive and upbeat!*
You can approach people by asking them if they want
"better options," "more choice," or a "healthy, no-cholesterol" or "environmental" option. By having a mainstream campaign, with the help of relatively few people,
we gathered over 1200 signatures (more than 25 percent
of the student population residing in the dorms) in only
two weeks.

Ask people that seem enthusiastic about the petition to
write a letter to the dining hall officials. We found that
these officials have little interaction with student concerns
pertaining to veganism. When letters started arriving, the
administrators heard the voice of the students and reacted
accordingly.

Meeting with the Administrators

Once you feel that enough petitions have been signed
and a sufficient amount of letters written, it is time to
contact administrators and set a meeting. We advise contacting them via writing and then follow up over the
telephone.

Once the meeting is set, the important thing to remember is *Come prepared!*

Bring a representative from each group involved in the campaign. You should prepare prior to the meeting to determine who will present each topic.

Then determine how the specific topics will be covered throughout the meeting. For example, we covered:

- Health issues (a no-cholesterol meal benefits all students).
- Freedom of choice (meat eaters also want a vegan option like other options (e.g., international food).
- Lower cost (the cost of making a vegan entree is less than the cost of making a meat entree).
- Increasing demand among dorm residents for a vegan option. The university should meet the demands of the increasing number of students who opt for a vegan option; this is when you should present the petition to show that more and more students would like a vegan entree at every meal.
- A concrete way in which the university can start implementing the vegan option. We strongly suggest that you present them with the Gold Plan published by the Physicians Committee for Responsible Medicine.
- Environmental option. People concerned with the environment will be very inclined to support a more plant-based diet.

Write an agenda for the meeting. This will let the administrator know that you are an organized campaign. Dress as well as possible without overdressing. Suits, ties, and business attire may be entirely appropriate. You want to show the administrator that you mean business!

Remind the administrator that this is a positive step for the university. The new vegan option will make the university look good. Remind her that you want to work with the university and that you can generate good publicity for it. Be helpful! Offer to assist the administrator in implementing the vegan plan. When you are finished, be sure to let the administrator know that you would like to meet with her again to follow up.

Let us know when you get vegan results!

Vegan Action, P.O. Box 4353, Berkeley, CA 94703.

Resources for Vegetarian Elders

American Association of Homes and Services for the Aging, 901 "E" Street NW, Suite 500, Washington, D.C. 20004-2037. Telephone: 1-800-827-4771. Organization of not-for-profit religious and fraternal nursing and rest homes.

American Health Care Association, 1201 "L" Street NW, Washington, D.C. 20005. Telephone: 202-842-4444. Association of large, for-profit nursing home chains (with some rest homes).

Long-Term Care Ombudsman, c/o National Citizens Coalition for Nursing Home Reform, 1224 "M" Street NW, Suite 301, Washington, D.C. 20005-5183. Telephone: 202-393-2018.

National Citizens Coalition for Nursing Home Reform, 1424 16th Street NW, Suite 202, Washington, D.C. 20036. Telephone: 202-332-2275.

Physicians Committee for Responsible Medicine (PCRM), 5100 Wisconsin Ave, NW, Suite 404, Washington, D.C. 20016. Telephone: 202-686-2210. Request an information packet including nutritional information and meal planning for institutional use.

Rocinante, 41, The Farm, Summertown, TN 38483. Attention: Stephen Gaskin. Telephone: 615-964-2519. Multi-age rural retirement community and midwife center.

Seventh Day Adventists, 12501 Old Columbia Pike, Silver Spring, MD 20904-6600. Nursing home list: Telephone: 301-680-6733, attention Alice Shu. Partial list of multigenerational vegetarian SDA communities: attention: Adventist Laymen's Services and Industries.

Sunset Hall, 2830 Francis Avenue, Los Angeles, CA 90005. Telephone: 213-387-5277. Rest home for radicals and free thinkers. Not vegetarian, but will accommodate.

Vegetarian Nutrition Dietetic Practice Group, American Dietetic Association, 216 W. Jackson Boulevard, Chicago, IL 60606. Telephone: 312-899-0040, extension 4602. For nutritional info or referral to the area coordinator of the VNDPG for your area, call toll-free 1-800-366-1655 (bilingual English/Spanish).

Vegetarian Resource Group, P.O. Box 1463, Baltimore, MD 21203. Telephone: 410-366-8343. Request an information packet including nutritional information and meal planning for institutional use.

DataBank

Appendix H:
Vegetarian Online Resources

If you're shopping for a commercial provider of online services, call the toll-free directory assistance operator (800-555-1212) for the toll-free number of one or more of the services you're considering. Ask if they have any promotional or trial offers, such as the first month free.

In addition to the Internet resources listed below, many of the commercial services have vegetarian recipes and discussion groups. For example, if you're on CompuServe, GO Vegetarian. If you're an America Onliner, check out Cooking Club, The Cupboard/Health and Nutrition Section, Vegetarian Lifestyle message folder. Or try searching the AOL member profiles for key words like "vegetarian" or "vegan" (or whatever else you're interested in). There are other resources within CompuServe and AOL, which you'll discover when you get into the aforementioned places. Other commercial providers should have similar vegetarian areas. If you already have another provider, you can send a message to the sysop asking where to find vegetarian resources. If you're trying to make a decision about which service to get, ask the ones you're shopping among how much vegetarian-related activity they have and where.

Commercial services all provide email, with which you can access at least some of the Internet resources below. There are also such nonprofit services as PeaceNet (peacenet@peacenet.org), EcoNet (econet@econet.org), AnimalsNet (animalsnet@igc.org), WomensNet (womensnet@womensnet.org), LaborNet (labornet@labornet.org), all of which have full Internet services. Call 415-442-0220 for info on any of these. An email to animalsnet@animal snet.org will get you an electronic brochure.

Vegetarian Internet Services

There are a number of books about the Internet, including *The Internet Starter Kit,* by Adam Engst; *Walking the World Wide Web,* by Shannon Turlington; and *The Internet Companion: A Beginner's Guide to Global Networking,* by Tracy LaQuey. This appendix has listings for USENET Newsgroups, Gopher, mailing lists, information via email, the World Wide Web, Internet Relay Chat, and anonymous FTP.

Thanks to Mark Wisdom for compiling and providing this list and giving permission to use it; to Bobbi Pasternak, who is compiling a list of online resources for the Vegetarian Resource Group; and to Geraint "Gedge" Edwards, VRG's European listings coordinator, for posting much of the information below on rec.food.veg. If you know of any other Internet vegetarian resources, please send them to Mark Wisdom <mwisdom@free.org>.

For an updated version of this guide, send email to: <mail-server@rtfm.mit.edu> with the following line in your message body: <send usenet/news.answers/vegetarian/guide/index>.

World Wide Web (WWW)

In order to access the Web directly, you must have a Web browser. Typical WWW browsers are Netscape, Mosaic, Lynx, and WWW. If you do not have access to WWW, but if you have access to telnet, then you can use WWW by telneting to a public WWW client, two of which are gopher.msu.edu and info.cern.ch. You can also telnet to www.njit.edu and log in as "WWW."

Animal Defense Network (ADN)

http://envirolink.org/adn/
    Home of the World Guide to Animal Rights. Part of the EnviroLink Network.

Animal Rights Resource Site (ARRS)

http://envirolink.org/arrs/
    Material on animal rights and vegetarianism.

ARK Online

http://www.teleport.com/~animals/
    "The online magazine for people who care about animals."

English Server Recipes Folder

http://english-server.hss.cmu.edu/Recipes.html
    Although not entirely vegetarian, much of it is vegetarian recipes. There are links to the Fat-Free archives and a few others. This server can also be reached via Gopher and FTP.

People for the Ethical Treatment of Animals (PETA)

http://envirolink.org/arrs/peta/index.html

Vegan Action

http://envirolink.org/arrs/va/home.html
Information on veganism, soft-copies of the *Vegan News,* animal derived ingredients and clothing lists.

Vegan Society UK

http://catless.ncl.ac.uk/Vegetarian/Orgs/VeganSocUK/vegansoc.html
Vegan Society leaflets, articles, list of local groups, and contacts.

Vegetarian Pages

http://catless.ncl.ac.uk/Vegetarian/
The main index to vegetarian resources on the Internet, and the home for hypertext documents relating to vegetarianism, including the hypertext version of this World Guide to Vegetarianism. It features links to many other Internet archives dealing with vegetarianism

Vegetarian Resource Group (VRG)

http://envirolink.org/arrs/VRG/home.html
Back issues of the *Vegetarian Journal,* articles, information, brochures, and newsletters on veganism, vegetarianism, nutrition, recipes, new products, travel, scientific studies, book and software reviews, animal rights.

Vegetarians International Voice for Animals (VIVA!)

http://catless.ncl.ac.uk/Vegetarian/Orgs/Viva/info.html
Accessible through the Vegetarian Society UK WWW page.

Vegetarian Society UK (VSUK)

http://catless.ncl.ac.uk/Vegetarian/Orgs/VegSocUK/
info html
    Contains the entire collection of VSUK infosheets.

Veggies Unite!

http://jalapeno.ucs.indiana.edu/cgi-bin/recipes/
    A searchable index of over 900 vegetarian recipes. Has
links to many nutrition and health sites.

* * *

Vegetarian organizations in North America:

MIT Vegetarian Support Group

http://www.mit.edu:8001/activities/vsg/home.html
    Massachusetts Institute of Technology, Cambridge,
Massachusetts, USA

Misissauga Vegetarian Association,
Ontario, Canada

http://www.interlog.com/~webweave/mva.html

Rice Vegetarian Club

http://www-ece.rice.edu/~andrew/rvc/rvc.html
    Rice University, Houston, Texas, USA

Triangle Vegetarian Society, North Carolina, USA

http://www.trinet.com/tonc/tvspage.html
    Includes Triangle area restaurant reviews.

Winnipeg Vegetarian Association, Manitoba, Canada

http://www.mbnet.mb.ca/~wva/index.html

WPI Vegetarian Society

http://www.wpi.edu/~veggies/
    Worcester Polytechnic Institute, Worcester, Massachusetts, USA

Vegetarian Products

Midland Harvest Burgers

http://emall.com/Harvest/Harvest1.html
    Nothing special, except that you can buy Midland Harvest burgers and other products from this site.

Naturally Yours

http://www.america.com/mall/store/naturally.html
    Sells grains and grain mills mostly. Seeds for sprouting, too.

Internet Relay Chat (IRC)

Two vegetarian discussion channels on IRC are "#veggies" and "#vegan."
    Geraint "Gedge" Edwards maintains a server/robot on #veggies called "VeganSrv" which maintains the channel when he's not on so that interested folks can get information on vegetarianism. Gedge is usually on in the (GMT) afternoons. #veggies has about 3 or 4 people chatting at times. Channels are created when people join them, so if you join "#veggie," and not "#veggies," you are not likely to see anyone else.

On IRC, people are known by their nicknames, so you must choose one with the "nick" command.

You can access IRC via the "irc" client program. If you don't have it available on your system, then you should be able to find it at your local friendly FTP site (archie searches on "ircII" should show you where to find it). Alternately you can telnet to a public IRC client (such as irc.demon.co.uk).

A typical session may include the following example commands:

```
/nick MyNickname
/join #veggies
/who #veggies (to see who is on #veggies)
/whois gedge (to see info about Gedge, if he's
currently on)
/msg gedge argh! (to ask Gedge for help, if he's
currently on)
/quit
```

All command lines must be prefixed with a "/". Anything not prefixed by a "/" will be sent to your current channel for all participants to see!

USENET Newsgroups

rec.food.veg

Posting/discussion of all vegetarian related subjects.

alt.food.fat-free

Posting/discussion related to fat-free foods/diet. Not entirely vegetarian.

rec.food.veg.cooking

A moderated newsgroup for the posting/discussion of vegetarian recipes, cooking information, nutrition, and other nonethical information.

talk.politics.animals

Posting/discussion of animal rights related subjects.

Mailing Lists

Many mailing lists are available in two formats: regular and digest. In the regular format, you get an email for every message posted. This is typically between five and fifty emails per day. In digest format, you get one email per day containing all the postings for the previous twenty-four hours.

AR-News

Related to AR-Talk. To subscribe, email ar-news request@cygnus.com with the following in your message body:
    sub ar-news <your first and last name here>
Availability of digest option: unknown.

AR-SFBay

News and announcements relating to animal rights and vegan/vegetarian issues and events for the greater San Francisco Bay area. Info on demonstrations, potlucks, presentations, and local news on animal issues. To subscribe, email to listproc@mellers1.psych.berkeley.edu with the following in your message body:
    sub ar-sfbay <your first and last name here>
Availability of digest option: unknown.

AR-Talk

A mailing list for the discussion of animal rights. Part of the Animal Rights Electronic Network (AREN). To subscribe, email to ar-talk-request@cygnus.com with the following in your message body:

> sub ar-talk <your first and last name here>

Availability of digest option: unknown.

East Bay Vegan News

A roughly bimonthly newsletter with news local to the San Francisco Bay Area. To subscribe, email to listproc-@mellers1.psych.berkeley.edu with the following in your message body:

> sub ebvn <your first and last name here>

Fat-Free

Intended for anyone following an extremely low-fat vegetarian diet, including followers of McDougall and Ornish. Only vegetarian recipes are permitted. The focus here is on the health and nutritional aspects of such diets, not ethical and ecological concerns. To subscribe, email to fatfree-request@hustle.rahul.net with one of the following two subject lines:

> ADD
> ADD DIGEST

BA-FatFree (San Francisco Bay Area) and Chicago Area FatFree

There are also local off-shoots of the FatFree mailing list for the San Francisco Bay Area and for the Chicago area. These discuss local issues and arrange get-togethers and potlucks. To subscribe to BA-FatFree, email to ba-fatfree-request@ hustle.rahul.net with "subscribe" in the message body.

To subscribe to the Chicago area list, write lee@bio 3.bsd.uchicago.edu or ekatman@midway.uchicago.edu for more details.

Macrobiotic

A list on macrobiotics. To subscribe, email to macrobiotic request@veda.is with the following in your message body:
    sub macrobiotic <your first and last name here>
Availability of digest option: unknown.

MaxLife

A list for those working toward a positive, healthy lifestyle while at the same time choosing to avoid heavy consumerism. It is for people who choose their activities with careful consideration to the pleasure they bring as well as all their costs. To subscribe, email to listserv@gibbs.oit.unc.edu with the following in your message body:
    sub maxlife <your first & last name here>
For the digest option, also add the following line:
    set maxlife digest

SNARE

Students Networking for Animal Rights Everywhere. A network of students involved with animal rights issues working to build alliances with other students around the world. To subscribe, email to owner-soar-list@ucs.indiana.edu.

Southern Ontario Vegetarian Mailing List

A list to discuss issues local to Southern Ontario, Canada, and to arrange get-togethers, restaurant outings, potlucks, etc. To subscribe, send your request to ontveg-request@csd.uwo.ca.

Vegan-L

A mailing list for vegans and aspiring vegans. To subscribe, email to listserv@templevm.bitnet with the following in your message body:

    sub vegan-l <your first and last name here>

For the digest option, also add the following line:

    set vegan-l digest

VegCMTE

For people who want to volunteer time to help VegLife keep up to date with journals, information files, recipes, etc. Also for those who want to work with their local vegetarian organizations, or who want to start their own. Contact Chuck Goelzer <cgl1@cornell.edu> for more info.

Veg-Cook

A mailing list where vegetarian cooks can exchange ideas and techniques. Subscribers also receive all posts to rec.food.veg.cooking. To subscribe, email to listserv@net com.com with the following in your message body:

    sub veg-cook <your first and last name here>

For the digest option, also add the following line:

    set veg-cook digest

Veggie

For the discussion of any aspect of vegetarianism, vegetarian lifestyle, or anything relevant to vegetarians. To subscribe, email to veggie-request@maths.bath.ac.uk with the following in your message body:

    sub veggie <your first & last name here>

For the digest option, also add the following line:

    set veggie digest

Veggies

For British vegetarian events/matters. Remarkably quiet. To subscribe, email to veggies-request@ncl.ac.uk with the following in your message body:
    sub veggies <your first & last name here>
Availability of digest option: unknown.

VegLife

Used to be called Granola. To subscribe, email to list serv@vtvm1.cc.vt.edu with the following in your message body:
    sub veglife <your first and last name here>
For the digest option, also add the following line:
    set veglife digest

VegPol-L

For discussing the book *The Sexual Politics of Meat* and other race/class/gender/veg issues. To subscribe, email to listproc@jefferson.village.virginia.edu with the following in your message body:
    sub vegpol-l <your first and last name here>

Anonymous FTP

When FTPing to an anonymous FTP site, use the user id "anonymous" and then enter your email address for the password.

bitnic.educom.edu:/nicbbs.391

Recipes. The recipes have a filename VEG_RECI and a file type of either DIGEST, INDEX, or VOLxxxxx.

cs.ubc.ca:/ftp/local/RECIPES/VEGETARIAN

Vegetarian recipes in Tex format.

Fat-Free Recipe Archive, 2 sites:

geod.emr.ca:/pub/Vegetarian
ftp.halcyon.com:/pub/recipes
    Large and growing archive of very lowfat and fat-free vegetarian recipes. Recipes range from simple to complex, easy to gourmet, mild to hot. There are recipes from cultures all around the world: Caribbean, Eastern European, South American, mainstream American, and so on. Indian cuisine is particularly well-represented in the collection. All the recipes are strictly vegetarian and contain no added fat and very little high-fat ingredients. Yet, the variety is astounding.

ftp.uu.net:/usenet/rec.food.recipes/vegan

Vegan recipes.

Great Cakes without Eggs, located at 2 sites:

oak.oakland.edu:SimTel/win3/food/great100.zip
ftp.demon.co.uk:pub/food/eggless
    Contains 216 recipes. In Winhelp hypertext format. Includes pictures. Simnel cake, gingerbread, fourteen different kinds of apple cake, Lebanese date cake, Jewish orange cake, Greek walnut cake, Texan Christmas cake, prune bread—you name it, it's here. About a quarter of the recipes are vegan, and the others are lacto-vegetarian. The measures are given in U.S. cup measures, Imperial, and Metric. This is a ShareWare software version of a successful paper book that is sold in England and Europe. Requires Windows 3.1+.

mthvax.cs.miami.edu:/pub/recipes/vegan

Perhaps a mirror of the VegLife site but with some differences.

news.answers Archives

rtfm.mit.edu:/pub/usenet/news.answers/vegetarian
news.answers archive site.
    Contains the latest officially posted copies of the World
Guide to Vegetarianism and the rec.food.veg FAQ.

SunSite Archives

sunsite.unc.edu:/pub/academic/medicine/alternative-healthcare
calypso-2.oit.unc.edu:/pub/academic/medicine/alternative-
healthcare
    Vegetarian recipes can be found under general/
nutrition/recipes.and.general-info/.Archives of rec.food.
veg. cooking, and a few other newsgroups can be found
under discussion-groups/newsgroups/.
    Also contains text files that may be of interest to vege-
tarians. SunSite is also accessible via Gopher, WWW,
WAIS, telnet, and ftpmail.

VegLife

cadadmin.cadlab.vt.edu:/VEGLIFE
    Several thousand vegetarian/vegan/fat-free recipes.
Vegetarian FAQs, information files, discussion archives,
etc. Userid "vegan" and password "guest" also work.
(128.173.53.239)

Vegetarian Resource Group Archives, 2 sites:

ftp.geod.emr.ca:/pub/Vegetarian/Articles
ftp.informatik.uni-hamburg.de:/pub/doc/vegetarian

VRG articles, newsletters, and pamphlets in electronic form. "The Vegetarian Game," an IBM-PC game by the VRG, is available from ftp.informatik.uni-hamburg.de.

Gopher

If you do not have access to Gopher, but have access to telnet, then you can use Gopher by telneting to a public Gopher client, two of which are gopher.msu.edu and panda.uiowa.edu.

english-server.hss.cmu.edu

Look under "Recipes." See listing under World Wide Web, above.

gopher.micro.umn.edu

Archives of rec.food.recipes. Look under "Fun & Games" or "Recipes." Four vegetarian subdirectories of recipes: vegan, lacto, ovo, and ovo-lacto.

usda.mannlib.cornell.edu

USDA Gopher site containing Lotus 123 spreadsheet format data regarding various kinds of farm production, food consumption, etc. A good place to verify some of the statistics used in arguments for vegetarianism.

Information by Email

The Fat-Free Recipe Archive

To get started, send the message "help" to archive-server@ halcyon.com. See listing under FTP sites below for more info. All requests are sent out compressed and unencoded.

The rec.food.veg Frequently Asked Questions (FAQ) Listing

For the latest officially posted copy of the rec.food.veg FAQ, email to mail-server@rtfm.mit.edu with the following line in your message body:
> send usenet/news.answers/vegetarian/faq

SunSite FTP by Email Service

Will FTP stuff from any site for you via email. Email to ftp mail@sunsite.unc.edu with "help" in the message body for instructions. See "Anonymous FTP Sites" above for examples of what is available.

Vegetarian Society U.K. Info Sheets

For help and an index, email to fileserv@salata.com with the following two lines in your message body:
> index
> help

The World Guide to Vegetarianism

For instructions on getting the latest officially posted copy of this guide via email, email to mail-server@rtfm.mit.edu with the following line in your message body:
> send usenet/news.answers/vegetarian/guide/index.

Notes

Chapter 1: Introduction

1. In popular usage, the word "diet" is often used to mean a restrictive meal plan in order to lose weight. More generally, however, it means simply whatever one eats. I use the term in this general sense, so that "vegetarian diet" means "vegetarian way of eating"—no more, no less.

Chapter 3: Vege-Vitality

1. Adapted from chart "Pesticide Residues in the U.S. Diet," *Diet for a New America,* p. 317, by John Robbins, Stillpoint Publishing, 1987. Previously adapted from Cornellussen, P. E., "Pesticide Residues in Total Diet," *Pesticides Monitoring Journal,* 2:140–152, 1969.

Chapter 6: Total Health

1. Chief Seattle, in a speech marking the forced transferal of ancestral Indian lands to the federal government, 1854, in *Power of the People: Active Nonviolence in the United States,* a written and pictorial history by Robert Cooney and Helen Michalowski. New Society Publishers, Philadelphia, Pennsylvania.

Chapter 8: Seed Beginings

1. Considered the most important Greek writer of the early Roman period, circa 46 B.C.–circa 120 A.D. The quote is from the Moralia.
2. Esme Wynne-Tyson, 1898–1972, English writer, in *The Philosophy of Compassion,* as quoted in *Fruits of Paradise: A Vegetarian Year-Book,* by Rebecca Hall, Simon & Schuster, 1963.
3. From the song "Water, Fire and Smoke," on the cassette album *In My Two Hands,* by Betsy Rose, ©1988 Paper Crane Music, P.O. Box 9538, Berkeley, CA 94709. $12 postpaid.
4. Vilmala Thaker, *Spirituality and Social Action: A Holistic Approach* (1984).
5. "The Slaughterer," *Isaac Bashevis Singer: The Collected Stories,* Farrar, Straus & Giroux, New York, NY., 1982.
6. Stephen Batchelor, describing the worldview of Shantideva in *Inquiring Mind,* Spring 1995.

Chapter 9: War and Peace

1. Sidebar in article "Green, Lean, and Not Mean," by Christine Beard, *Green Consensus,* Aug/Sept 1994.
2. Copied by the author from the wall of a Buddhist temple in Taiwan, circa 1975.

Chapter 11: Eating the World

1. Some growth can be achieved through more effective use of resources: organizational reforms and those technological advances not requiring increased resource use. But much economic growth involves increased consumption of resources and/or other negative ecological impacts.
2. From *Faslane Focus* newsletter, U.K., circa 1987.

Chapter 12: Blood on the Tongue

1. *Farmer and Stockbreeder,* Jan. 30, 1962. Quoted in *Diet for a New America,* by John Robbins, Stillpoint Publishing, Walpole, NH, 1987. Page 53.

2. "Raising Pigs by the Calendar at Maplewood Farm," *Hog Farm Management,* September 1976. Article by J. Byrnes. Quoted in *Diet for a New America,* pages 8–82.

3. *National Hog Farmer*, March 1978, page 27. Article by L. Taylor. (Quoted in *Diet for a New America*, page 85.)

4. *Diet for a New America* by John Robbins, Stillpoint Publishing, Walpole, NH, 1987. Page 82.

Chapter 13: The Vegan Alternative

1. From "Truth or Dairy," video produced by the Vegan Society U.K. Available in U.S. format from the American Vegan Society (see Appendix C: Organizations).

2. Colin Campbell, interviewed in "The Latest from the China Diet and Health Study," *Good Medicine,* Physicians Committee for Responsible Medicine.Vol. III, No. 3. Summer 1994.

Chapter 14: Do It!

1. from the poem "Song," by Deena Metzger, published in *Looking for the Faces of God*, Parallax Press, Berkeley, CA 1989.

Chapter 15: Getting There

1. From the song "Taste and See," by Betsy Rose on the cassette album *In My Two Hands*, "written for a women's ritual reclaiming Eden and the apple." Copyright © 1988 Paper Crane Music, P.O. Box 9538, Berkeley, CA 94709. $12 postpaid.

Chapter 16: Icons

1. *Saccharomyces cerevisiae* or Red Star Nutritional Yeast T6635. Nonfermenting yeast has a cheesy taste, unlike brewers yeast or torula (*candida utilis*), which should not be substituted.

2. Sesame salt is made by roasting eight to twelve parts of sesame seeds in a skillet over medium heat, stirring constantly to prevent scorching; adding one part salt; and blending in a food processor until 90 percent of the seeds are powdered but 10 percent are still whole. Allow to cool in open air before bottling. Use in place of salt.

Chapter 17: Vege-Babes

1. *Food for Life* by Neal Barnard, M.D., founder of Physicians Committee for Responsible Medicine. Harmony Books, New York, 1993.

Chapter 20: Money Talks

1. From *The Extended Circle: An Anthology of Humane Thought,* by Jon Wynne-Tyson. Sphere Books., Ltd., London, 1990.
2. Connie Salamone, *Majority Report 72.* From *The Extended Circle.*

Index